KETO CHAFFLE COOKBOOK

90 Quick & Easy Low-Carb Ketogenic Diet Recipes. How to Cook Delicious Keto Waffle for Weight Loss and Boost Your Metabolism, from Dessert to Complete Meal

EMILY COOK

Table of Contents

CHAPTER-1:
INTRODUCTION

INTRODUCTION

1.1 WHAT ARE CHAFFLES?

In simple terms, a chaffle is a waffle made up of cheese and eggs. Chaffles made from cheese and eggs taste like ordinary waffles.

The simplest definition of a chaffle is a low-carb waffle with cheese being themain ingredient.

Instead of using flour, different cheeses like mozzarella, cheddar, and Colby jack are used in chaffles to give them texture and shape life waffles.
They're so popular on low-carb and keto lifestyles because they literally taste like a waffle – crunch and all.

1.2 WHAT ARE THE TYPICAL INGREDIENTS IN A CHAFFLE?

Some most commonly used ingredients like cheese, eggs, vanilla, coffee, cinnamon almond flour, and low carb sweeteners like stevia are used in sweet chaffles.

Salt cheeses like cheddar or jack are commonly mixedwith Italian seasoning, garlic powder, salt, pizza sauce, sesame seeds, bagel seasoning in savory chaffles.
Some vegetables like zucchini, spinach, cauliflower, pumpkin spices are also used in savory chaffles.

Instead of using egg, flaxseed egg or chia seed egg is used in vegan chaffles with low carb vegan cheese.

1.3 HOW DO YOU MAKE A CHAFFLE?

You can easily make chaffles by mixing chaffle ingredients in a mixing bowl. Make sure that all ingredients arethoroughly mixed together. Once the batter is mixed, pour it intoa preheated greased waffle machine and cook in a given time.

1.4 TOOLS FOR MAKINGCHAFFLES

Measuring cups, spoons, mixing bowl and a spatula and, of course, good chaffle maker are used for making chaffles.

1.5 TASTE OF CHAFFLE

A chaffle tastes like a waffle! Chaffles are crunchy from the outside and soft from the inside.Chaffles can be made froma variety of ingredients from savory to sweet, vegan to vegetarian.

Chaffles are keto-friendly snacks. Cheese is the base ingredient so they are low in carbohydrates and high in fat.

Chaffles can be used for breakfasts, as bread replacements for lunchtime sandwiches, snacks, dessert and for dinner.

1.6 TIME TO MAKE A CHAFFLE

Chaffles can be made in 5-15 minutes, dependingon the quantity you want.

1.7 VEGAN CHAFFLE

Chaffles can be made for people with a vegan lifestyle. Vegan, low carb cheese can be used instead of regular cheese.
Flaxseed and Chia seed are options instead of using eggs.

1.8 ALMOND FLOUR/ COCONUT FLOUR IN CHAFFLE

Almond flour or coconut flour helps to bind ingredients together and gives texture to chaffles.
Almond flour/ coconut flours give chaffles a bread-like texture.

TIPS FOR DELICIOUS AND
CRISPY CHAFFLE

- Start making chaffles with the basic mini waffle maker.
- Don't overfill the mini waffle maker, use 1/8-1/4 cup of batter
- Spray waffle maker with coconut oil before cooking for a crispy texture.
- A layer of cheese before and after the batter in maker can give it a crispy texture. Sprinkling 1 tbsp. cheese before and after the batter in the waffle maker may help to release chaffles easily from waffle maker and makes chaffles crunchy.
- Always preheat waffle maker before cookingso that it will be less sticky and easier to clean up.
- Instead of using the whole egg, egg whites can be used in chaffles to give it no eggy flavor.
- Let chaffles stand at room temperature to give it a crunchy texture.
- Do not fill waffle maker with more than 1/4 cup of TOTAL ingredients at a time.
- Use a wet paper towel to clean up the waffle maker when the waffle iron is warm to clean it easily.
- Use a toothbrush to clean inside the waffle machine.
- Use shredded cheese instead of a slice in the batter. It helps to mix all ingredients well.

WAFFLE MAKER TYPES AND USES

1. CLASSIC ROUND WAFFLE MAKER

This waffle maker is also called an American waffle maker. This waffle maker is round in shape with cast iron varieties. These are used for round shape waffles.

2. BELGIAN WAFFLE MAKER

This is the most popular type of waffle maker. This waffle maker makes waffles that are quite thick. The thickness ranges from 1" to 1 ½", and the beauty of waffles is they are crispy outside and soft inside.

3. HEART WAFFLE MAKER

Shaped waffle makers are most popular for kids' snacks.

4. SQUARE WAFFLE MAKER

The square is the most popular shape along with the circle and the waffles are usually cut into four smaller pieces. However, with the Belgian waffle maker of this shape, it is possible to get a square waffle that isn't as thick as the European type.

5. WAFFLE IRON

This waffle iron is used to make waffles without a waffle machine.It is put on a stove and is commonly referred to as a stovetop waffle maker.

6. DASH MINI WAFFLE MAKER

This waffle maker is used to make mini Waffles.They are in round shape and mini square shapes are also available in the market.

CHAFFLES WITHOUT WAFFLE MAKER

Delicious chaffles can be made without a waffle iron or waffler iron.These chaffles will be as crispy as in regular waffle maker.

Some people havetried different experiments and made chaffles without any waffle maker, perhaps they do not like most of the kitchen appliances. So,there might be so many reasons why people do not buy a waffle iron.

You just need a grill and waffle mold to convert your chaffle batter into tasty chaffles. Both methods are perfect to make waffles.

MAKE CHAFFLES USING GRILL METHOD

Chaffles made with the grill method look like pancakes but they are still chaffles. Chaffles made on the grill are crispy from outside and inside is airy just like regular chaffles.

The regular batter that is used from waffle maker can be used in the grill Method. Grease your grill then pour the batter in the greased grill. Cook for about 2-3 minutes, flip and again cook for 1-2 minutes on the grill.

MAKE CHAFFLES USING A SILICONE WAFFLE MOLD

This is another way of making Chaffles without a waffle iron or grill. You can make almost 16 waffles using both sets of a silicone waffle mold.

In this method, mold is filled with chaffle batter and then baked in a preheated oven for about 10-15minutes.

CHAPTER-2:
BEGINNER CHAFFLE RECIPE

SIMPLE& BEGINNER CHAFFLE

Prep Time: 5 min
Cooking Time: 5 min
Total Time: 10 min
Servings: 2

INGREDIENTS
- 1 large egg
- 1/2 cup mozzarella cheese, shredded
- Cooking spray

DIRECTIONS
1. Switch on your waffle maker.
2. Beat the egg with a fork in a small mixing bowl.
3. Once the egg is beaten, add the mozzarella and mix well.
4. Spray the waffle makerwith cooking spray.
5. Pour the chaffles mixture in a preheated waffle maker and let it cook for about 2-3 minutes.
6. Once the chaffles are cooked, carefully remove them from the maker and cook the remaining batter.
7. Serve hot with coffee and enjoy!

NUTRITIONAL INFORMATION

Amount per serving 42 g

Total Calories	120 kcal
Fats	7.9 g
Protein	10.42 g
Net Carbs	0.93 g
Fiber	0 g
Starch	0 g

Protein: 36% 42 kcal
Fat: 60% 71 kcal
Carbohydrates: 4% 5 kcal

CHAFFLES WITH ALMOND FLOUR

Prep Time: 5 min
Cooking Time: 5 min
Total Time: 10 min
Servings: 4

INGREDIENTS
- 2 large eggs
- 1/4 cup almond flour
- 3/4 tsp baking powder
- 1 cup cheddar cheese, shredded
- Cooking spray

DIRECTIONS
1. Switch on your waffle maker and grease with cooking spray.
2. Beat eggs with almond flour and baking powder in a mixing bowl.
3. Once the eggs and cheese are mixed together, add in cheese and mix again.
4. Pour 1/4 cup of the batter in the dash mini waffle maker and close the lid.
5. Cook chaffles for about 2-3 minutes until crispy and cooked
6. Repeat with the remaining batter
7. Carefully transfer the chafflesto plate.
8. Serve with almonds and enjoy!

NUTRITIONAL INFORMATION

Amount per serving 68 g

Total Calories	222 kcal
Fats	18.01 g
Protein	12.97 g
Net Carbs	1.32 g
Fiber	1.1 g
Starch	0.06 g

Protein: 23% 52 kcal
Fat: 72% 159 kcal
Carbohydrates: 5% 11 kcal

BASIC CHAFFLES RECIPE FOR SANDWICHES

Prep Time: 5 min
Cooking Time: 5 min
Total Time: 10 min
Servings: 2

INGREDIENTS
- 1/2 cup mozzarella cheese, shredded
- 1 large egg
- 2 tbsps. almond flour
- 1/2 tsp psyllium husk powder
- 1/4 tsp baking powder

DIRECTIONS
1. Grease your Belgian waffle maker with cooking spray.
2. Beat the egg with a fork; once the egg is beaten, add almond flour, husk powder, and baking powder.
3. Add cheesetothe egg mixture and mix until combined.
4. Pour batter in the center of Belgian waffle and close the lid.
5. Cook chaffles for about 2-3 minutes until well cooked.
6. Carefully transfer the chaffles to plate.
7. The chaffles are perfect for a sandwich base.

NUTRITIONAL INFORMATION

Amount per serving 74 g

Total Calories	211 kcal
Fats	15.11 g
Protein	15.22 g
Net Carbs	1.27 g
Fiber	1.65 g
Starch	0.1 g

Protein: 29% 60 kcal
Fat: 63% 132 kcal
Carbohydrates: 8% 18 kcal

GARLIC CHAFFLES

Prep Time: 5 min
Cooking Time: 5 min
Total Time: 10 min
Servings: 4

INGREDIENTS
- 1/2 cup mozzarella cheese, shredded
- 1/3 cup cheddar cheese
- 1 large egg
- ½ tbsp. garlic powder
- 1/2 tsp Italian seasoning
- 1/4 tsp baking powder

DIRECTIONS
1. Switch on your waffle maker and lightly grease your waffle maker with a brush.
2. Beat the egg with garlic powder, Italian seasoning and baking powder in a small mixing bowl.
3. Add mozzarella cheese and cheddar cheese tothe egg mixture and mix well.
4. Pour half of the chaffles batter into the middle of your waffle iron and close the lid.
5. Cook chaffles for about 2-3 minutes until crispy.

6. Once cooked, remove chaffles from the maker.
7. Sprinkle garlic powder on top and enjoy!

NUTRITIONAL INFORMATION

Amount per serving 42 g

Total Calories	114 kcal
Fats	7.71 g
Protein	8.95 g
Net Carbs	1.62 g
Fiber	0.2 g
Starch	0 g

Protein: 32% 36 kcal
Fat: 61% 69 kcal
Carbohydrates: 7% 7 kcal

CINNAMON POWDER CHAFFLES

Prep Time: 5 min
Cooking Time: 5 min
Total Time: 10 min
Servings: 2

INGREDIENTS
- 1 large egg
- 3/4 cup cheddar cheese, shredded
- 2 tbsps. coconut flour
- 1/2 tbsps. coconut oil melted
- 1 tsp. stevia
- 1/2 tsp cinnamon powder
- 1/2 tsp vanilla extract
- 1/2 tsp psyllium husk powder
- 1/4 tsp baking powder

DIRECTIONS
1. Switch on your waffle maker.
2. Grease your waffle maker with cooking spray and heat up on medium heat.
3. In a mixing bowl, beat egg withcoconut flour, oil, stevia, cinnamon powder, vanilla, husk powder, and baking powder.
4. Once the egg is beaten well, add in cheeseand mix again.
5. Pour half of the waffle batter into the middle of your waffle iron and close the lid.
6. Cook chaffles for about 2-3 minutes until crispy.

17

7. Once chaffles are cooked, carefully remove them from the maker.
8. Serve with keto hot chocolate and enjoy!

NUTRITIONAL INFORMATION

Amount per serving 83 g

Total Calories	246 kcal
Fats	19.47 g
Protein	15.13 g
Net Carbs	1.05 g
Fiber	0.5 g
Starch	0 g

Protein: 25% 62 kcal
Fat: 72% 175 kcal
Carbohydrates: 3% 7 kcal

PUMPKIN CHAFFLES

Prep Time: 5 min
Cooking Time: 5 min
Total Time: 10 min
Servings: 2

INGREDIENTS
- 1/2 oz. cream cheese
- 1 large egg
- 1/2 cup cheddar cheese, shredded
- 2 tbsps. pumpkin puree
- 1 tsp. stevia
- 3 tsps. coconut flour
- 1/2 tbsps. pumpkin pie spice
- 1/2 tsp vanilla extract
- 1/4 tsp baking powder

DIRECTIONS
1. Grease your Belgian waffle maker with cooking spray and switch it on.
2. Crack the egg in a mixing bowl containingcoconut flour, pumpkin spice, stevia, pumpkin spice, vanilla extract, and baking powder. Mix thoroughly.
3. Once the ingredients are mixed together with egg, add in cheese and mix again.

4. Pour half of the chaffles batter into the middle of your waffle iron and close the lid.
5. Cook chaffles for about 2-3 minutes until cooked and light golden.
6. Repeat with the remaining batter
7. Once chaffles are cooked, remove from the maker.
8. Serve with BLT coffee and enjoy!

NUTRITIONAL INFORMATION

Amount per serving 111 g

Total Calories	260 kcal
Fats	20.93 g
Protein	12.33 g
Net Carbs	2.4 g
Fiber	1.6 g
Starch	0.02 g

Protein: 19% 50 kcal
Fat: 72% 185 kcal
Carbohydrates: 9% 23 kcal

SPICY JALAPENO & BACON CHAFFLES

Prep Time: 5 min
Cooking Time: 5 min
Total Time: 10 min
Servings: 2

INGREDIENTS
- 1 oz. cream cheese
- 1 large egg
- 1/2 cup cheddar cheese
- 2 tbsps. bacon bits
- 1/2 tbsp. jalapenos
- 1/4 tsp baking powder

DIRECTIONS
1. Switch on your waffle maker.
2. Grease your waffle maker with cooking spray and let it heat up.
3. Mix together egg and vanilla extract in a bowl first.
4. Add baking powder, jalapenos and bacon bites.
5. Add in cheese last and mix together.
6. Pour the chaffles batter intothe maker and cook the chaffles for about 2-3 minutes.
7. Once chaffles are cooked, remove from the maker.

8. Serve hot and enjoy!

NUTRITIONAL INFORMATION

Amount per serving 87 g

Total Calories	248 kcal
Fats	19.44 g
Protein	14.39g
Net Carbs	2.01 g
Fiber	0.9 g
Starch	0 g

Protein: 24% 59 kcal
Fat: 70% 175 kcal
Carbohydrates: 6% 15 kcal

RASPBERRIES CHAFFLES

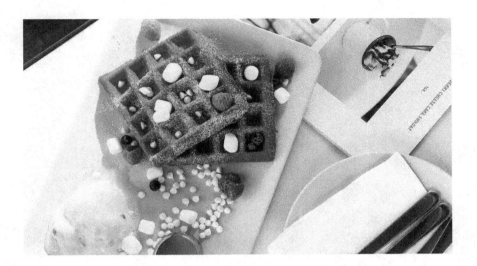

Prep Time: 5 min
Cooking Time: 5 min
Total Time: 10 min
Servings: 2

INGREDIENTS
- 1 egg
- 1/2 cup mozzarella cheese, shredded
- 1 tbsp. almond flour
- 1/4 cup raspberry puree
- 1 tbsp. coconut flour for topping

DIRECTIONS
1. Preheat your waffle makerin line with the manufacturer's instructions.
2. Grease your waffle maker with cooking spray.
3. Mix together egg, almond flour, and raspberry purée.
4. Add cheese and mix until well combined.
5. Pour batter intothe waffle maker.
6. Close the lid.
7. Cook for about 3-4 minutes or until waffles are cooked and not soggy.
8. Once cooked, remove from the maker.
9. Sprinkle coconut flour on top and enjoy!

NUTRITIONAL INFORMATION

Amount per serving 92 g

Total Calories	231 kcal
Fats	16.71 g
Protein	15.2 g
Net Carbs	1.56 g
Fiber	2.9 g
Starch	0.1 g

Protein: 26% 60 kcal
Fat: 63% 145 kcal
Carbohydrates: 11% 25 kcal

KETO COCOA CHAFFLES

Prep Time: 5 min
Cooking Time: 5 min
Total Time: 10 min
Servings: 2

INGREDIENTS
* 1 large egg
* 1/2 cup shredded cheddar cheese
* 1 tbsp. cocoa powder
* 2 tbsps. almond flour

DIRECTIONS
1. Preheat your round waffle maker on medium-high heat.
2. Mix together egg, cheese, almond flour, cocoa powder and vanilla in a small mixing bowl.
3. Pour chaffles mixture into the center of the waffle iron.
4. Close the waffle maker and let cook for 3-5 minutes or until waffle is golden brown and set.
5. Carefully remove chaffles from the waffle maker.
6. Serve hot and enjoy!

NUTRITIONAL INFORMATION

Amount per serving 58 g

Total Calories	250 kcal
Fats	20.86 g
Protein	12.77 g
Net Carbs	1.97 g
Fiber	2.6 g
Starch	0.1 g

Protein: 20% 49 kcal
Fat: 73% 183 kcal
Carbohydrates: 7% 17 kcal

SIMPLE CHAFFLE TOAST

Prep Time: 5 min
Cooking Time: 5 min
Total Time: 10 min
Servings: 2

INGREDIENTS
- 1 large egg
- 1/2 cup shredded cheddar cheese

FOR TOPPING
1 egg
3-4 spinach leaves
¼ cup boil and shredded chicken

DIRECTIONS
1. Preheat your square waffle maker on medium-high heat.
2. Mix together egg and cheese in a bowl and make two chaffles in a chaffle maker
3. Once chaffle are cooked, carefully remove them from the maker.
4. Serve with spinach, boiled chicken, and fried egg.
5. Serve hot and enjoy!

NUTRITIONAL INFORMATION

Amount per serving 120 g

Total Calories	256 kcal
Fats	17.04 g
Protein	23.57 g
Net Carbs	0.68 g
Fiber	0 g
Starch	0.1 g

Protein: 39% 99 kcal
Fat: 60% 153 kcal
Carbohydrates: 1% 3 kcal

CHAPTER-3:
BREAKFAST CHAFFLE RECIPES

MORNING CHAFFLES WITH BERRIES

Prep Time: 5 min
Cooking Time: 5 min
Total Time: 10 min
Servings: 4

INGREDIENTS
- 1 cup egg whites
- 1 cup cheddar cheese, shredded
- ¼ cup almond flour
- ¼ cup heavy cream

TOPPING
- 4 oz. raspberries
- 4 oz. strawberries.
- 1 oz. keto chocolate flakes
- 1 oz. feta cheese.

DIRECTIONS
1. Preheat your square waffle maker and grease with cooking spray.
2. Beat egg white in a small bowl with flour.
3. Add shredded cheese to the egg whites and flour mixture and mix well.
4. Add cream and cheese tothe egg mixture.
5. Pour Chaffles batter in a waffle maker and close the lid.
6. Cook chaffles for about 4 minutes until crispy and brown.

7. Carefully remove chaffles from the maker.
8. Serve with berries, cheese, and chocolate on top.
9. Enjoy!

NUTRITIONAL INFORMATION

Amount per serving 110 g

Total Calories	243 kcal
Fats	18.51 g
Protein	16.6 g
Total Carbs	0.8 g
Fiber	1.1 g
Starch	0.06 g

Protein: 28% 68 kcal
Fat: 67% 163 kcal
Carbohydrates: 5% 12 kcal

CHAFFLES BREAKFAST BOWL

Prep Time: 10 min
Cooking Time: 5 min
Total Time: 15 min
Servings: 2

INGREDIENTS
- 1 egg
- 1/2 cup cheddar cheese shredded
- pinch of Italian seasoning
- 1 tbsp. pizza sauce

TOPPING
- 1/2 avocado sliced
- 2 eggs boiled
- 1 tomato, halves
- 4 oz. fresh spinach leaves

DIRECTIONS
1. Preheat yourwaffle maker and grease with cooking spray.
2. Crack an egg in a small bowl and beat with Italian seasoning and pizza sauce.
3. Add shredded cheese to the egg and spices mixture.
4. Pour 1 tbsp. shredded cheese in a waffle maker and cook for 30 sec.
5. Pour Chaffles batter inthe waffle maker and close the lid.

6. Cook chaffles for about 4 minutes until crispy and brown.
7. Carefully remove chaffles from the maker.
8. Serve on the bed of spinach with boil egg, avocado slice, and tomatoes.
9. Enjoy!

NUTRITIONAL INFORMATION

Amount per serving 276 g

Total Calories	339 kcal
Fats	25.54 g
Protein	7.16 g
Net Carbs	2.15 g
Fiber	5.6 g
Starch	0.06 g

Protein: 23% 77 kcal
Fat: 66% 222 kcal
Carbohydrates: 11% 39 kcal

CRISPY CHAFFLES WITH SAUSAGE

Prep Time: 5 min
Cooking Time: 10 min
Total Time: 15 min
Servings: 2

INGREDIENTS
- 1/2 cup cheddar cheese
- 1/2 tsp. baking powder
- 1/4 cup egg whites
- 2 tsp. pumpkin spice
- 1 egg, whole
- 2 chicken sausage
- 2 slice bacon
- salt and pepper to taste
- 1 tsp. avocado oil

DIRECTIONS
1. Mix together all ingredients in a bowl.
2. Allow batter to sit while waffle iron warms.
3. Spray waffle iron with nonstick spray.
4. Pour batter in the waffle maker and cook according to the directions of the manufacturer.

5. Meanwhile, heat oil in a pan and fry the egg, according to your choice and transfer it toa plate.
6. In the same pan, fry bacon slice and sausage on medium heat for about 2-3 minutes until cooked.
7. Once chaffles are cooked thoroughly, remove them from the maker.
8. Serve with fried egg, bacon slice, sausages and enjoy!

NUTRITIONAL INFORMATION

Amount per serving 146 g

Total Calories	384 kcal
Fats	31.82 g
Protein	20.77 g
Net Carbs	2.28 g
Fiber	0.3 g
Starch	0 g

Protein: 22% 86 kcal
Fat: 74% 286 kcal
Carbohydrates: 3% 12 kcal

MINI BREAKFAST CHAFFLES

Prep Time: 5 min
Cooking Time: 15 min
Total Time: 30 min
Servings: 3

INGREDIENTS
- 6 tsp coconut flour
- 1 tsp stevia
- 1/4 tsp baking powder
- 2 eggs
- 3 oz. cream cheese
- 1/2. tsp vanilla extract

Topping
- 1 egg
- 6 slice bacon
- 2 oz. Raspberries for topping
- 2 oz. Blueberries for topping
- 2 oz. Strawberries for topping

DIRECTIONS

1. Heat up your square waffle maker and grease with cooking spray.
2. Mix together coconut flour, stevia, egg, baking powder, cheese and vanilla in mixing bowl.
3. Pour ½ of chaffles mixture in a waffle maker.
4. Close the lid and cook the chaffles for about 3-5 minutes.
5. Meanwhile, fry bacon slices in pan on medium heat for about 2-3 minutes until cooked and transfer themto plate.
6. In the same pan, fry eggs one by one in the leftover grease of bacon.
7. Once chaffles are cooked, carefully transferthem toplate.
8. Serve with fried eggs and bacon slice and berries on top.
9. Enjoy!

NUTRITIONAL INFORMATION

Amount per serving 218 g

Total Calories	462 kcal
Fats	38.44 g
Protein	18.05 g
Net Carbs	0.93 g
Fiber	2 g
Starch	0.01 g

Protein: 16% 75 kcal
Fat: 75% 346 kcal
Carbohydrates: 9% 41 kcal

CRISPY CHAFFLES WITH EGG & ASPARAGUS

Prep Time: 5 min
Cooking Time: 10 min
Total Time: 15 min
Servings: 1

INGREDIENTS
- 1 egg
- 1/4 cup cheddar cheese
- 2 tbsps. almond flour
- ½ tsp. baking powder

TOPPING
- 1 egg
- 4-5 stalks asparagus
- 1 tsp avocado oil

DIRECTIONS
1. Preheat waffle maker to medium-high heat.
2. Whisk together egg, mozzarella cheese, almond flour, and baking powder
3. Pour chaffles mixture into the center of the waffle iron. Close the waffle maker and let cook for 3-5 minutes or until waffle is golden brown and set.
4. Remove chaffles from the waffle maker and serve.
5. Meanwhile, heat oil in a nonstick pan.

6. Once the pan is hot, fry asparagus for about 4-5 minutes until golden brown.
7. Poach the egg in boil water for about 2-3 minutes.
8. Once chaffles are cooked, remove from the maker.
9. Serve chaffles with the poached egg and asparagus.

NUTRITIONAL INFORMATION

Amount per serving 184 g

Total Calories	327 kcal
Fats	25.3 g
Protein	20.68 g
Net Carbs	1.82 g
Fiber	1.5 g
Starch	0.02 g

Protein: 26% 85 kcal
Fat: 69% 226 kcal
Carbohydrates: 5% 16 kcal

COCONUT CHAFFLES

Prep Time: 5 min
Cooking Time: 5 min
Total Time: 10 min
Servings: 2

INGREDIENTS
- 1 egg
- 1 oz. cream cheese,
- 1 oz. cheddar cheese
- 2 tbsps. coconut flour
- 1 tsp. stevia
- 1 tbsp. coconut oil, melted
- 1/2 tsp. coconut extract
- 2 eggs, soft boil for serving

DIRECTIONS
1. Heat you mini Dash waffle maker and grease with cooking spray.
2. Mix together all chaffles ingredients in a bowl.
3. Pour chaffle batter in a preheated waffle maker.
4. Close the lid.
5. Cook chaffles for about 2-3 minutes until golden brown.
6. Serve with boil egg and enjoy!

NUTRITIONAL INFORMATION

Amount per serving 78 g

Total Calories	153 kcal
Fats	13.35 g
Protein	7.41 g
Net Carbs	0.08 g
Fiber	0.1 g
Starch	0 g

Protein: 21% 32 kcal
Fat: 76% 117 kcal
Carbohydrates: 3% 4 kcal

AVOCADO CHAFFLE TOAST

Prep Time: 5 min
Cooking Time: 10 min
Total Time: 15 min
Servings: 3

INGREDIENTS
- 4 tbsps. avocado mash
- 1/2 tsp lemon juice
- 1/8 tsp salt
- 1/8 tsp black pepper
- 2 eggs
- 1/2 cup shredded cheese

For serving
- 3 eggs
- ½ avocado thinly sliced
- 1 tomato, sliced

DIRECTIONS
1. Mash avocado mash with lemon juice, salt, and black pepper in mixing bowl, until well combined.
2. In a small bowl beat egg and pour eggs in avocado mixture and mix well.
3. Switch on Waffle Maker to pre-heat.

4. Pour 1/8 of shredded cheese in a waffle maker and then pour ½ of egg and avocado mixture and then 1/8 shredded cheese.
5. Close the lid and cook chaffles for about 3 - 4 minutes.
6. Repeat with the remaining mixture.
7. Meanwhile, fry eggs in a pan for about 1-2 minutes.
8. For serving, arrange fried egg on chaffle toast with avocado slice and tomatoes.
9. Sprinkle salt and pepper on top and enjoy!

NUTRITIONAL INFORMATION

Amount per serving 140 g

Total Calories	250 kcal
Fats	19.26 g
Protein	15.42 g
Net Carbs	0.79 g
Fiber	2.7 g
Starch	0.04 g

Protein: 26% 66 kcal
Fat: 67% 169 kcal
Carbohydrates: 6% 15 kcal

CAJUN & FEETA CHAFFLES

Prep Time: 5 min
Cooking Time: 10 min
Total Time: 30 min
Servings: 1

INGREDIENTS
- 1 egg white
- 1/4 cup shredded mozzarella cheese
- 2 tbsps. almond flour
- 1 tsp Cajun Seasoning

FOR SERVING
- 1 egg
- 4 oz. feta cheese
- 1 tomato, sliced

DIRECTIONS
1. Whisk together egg, cheese, and seasoning in a bowl.
2. Switch on and grease waffle maker with cooking spray.
3. Pour batter in a preheated waffle maker.
4. Cook chaffles for about 2-3 minutes until the chaffle is cooked through.
5. Meanwhile, fry the egg in a non-stick pan for about 1-2 minutes.
6. For serving set fried egg on chaffles with feta cheese and tomatoes slice.

NUTRITIONAL INFORMATION

Amount per serving 217 g

Total Calories	423 kcal
Fats	30.61 g
Protein	27.88 g
Net Carbs	1.39 g
Fiber	0.8 g
Starch	0.01 g

Protein: 28% 119 kcal
Fat: 64% 270 kcal
Carbohydrates: 7% 31 kcal

GARLIC AND PARSLEY CHAFFLES

Prep Time: 10 min
Cooking Time: 5 min
Total Time: 15 min
Servings: 1

INGREDIENTS
- 1 large egg
- 1/4 cup cheese mozzarella
- 1 tsp. coconut flour
- ¼ tsp. baking powder
- ½ tsp. garlic powder
- 1 tbsp. minced parsley

For Serving
- 1 Poach egg
- 4 oz. smoked salmon

DIRECTIONS
1. Switch on yourDash miniwaffle maker and let it preheat.
2. Grease waffle maker with cooking spray.
3. Mix together egg, mozzarella, coconut flour, baking powder, and garlic powder, parsley to a mixing bowl until combined well.
4. Pour batter in circle chaffle maker.
5. Close the lid.

6. Cook for about 2-3 minutes or until the chaffles are cooked.
7. Serve with smoked salmon and poached egg.
8. Enjoy!

NUTRITIONAL INFORMATION

Amount per serving 195 g

Total Calories	316 kcal
Fats	17.8 g
Protein	33.35 g
Net Carbs	2.53 g
Fiber	0.4 g
Starch	0 g

Protein: 45% 140 kcal
Fat: 51% 160 kcal
Carbohydrates: 4% 14 kcal

DELICIOUS RASPBERRIESTACO CHAFFLES

Prep Time: 5 min
Cooking Time: 15 min
Total Time: 20 min
Servings: 1

INGREDIENTS
- 1 egg white
- 1/4 cup jack cheese, shredded
- 1/4 cup cheddar cheese, shredded
- 1 tsp coconut flour
- 1/4 tsp baking powder
- 1/2 tsp stevia

For Topping
- 4 oz. raspberries
- 2 tbsps. coconut flour
- 2 oz. unsweetened raspberry sauce

DIRECTIONS
1. Switch on yourround Waffle Maker and grease it with cooking spray once it is hot.
2. Mix together all chaffle ingredients in a bowl and combine with a fork.
3. Pour chaffle batter in a preheated maker and close the lid.

4. Roll the taco chaffle around using a kitchen roller, set it aside and allow it to set for a few minutes.
5. Once the taco chaffle is set, remove from the roller.
6. Dip raspberries in sauce and arrange on taco chaffle.
7. Drizzle coconut flour on top.
8. Enjoy raspberries taco chaffle with keto coffee.

NUTRITIONAL INFORMATION

Amount per serving 99 g

Total Calories	272 kcal
Fats	21.06 g
Protein	18.46 g
Net Carbs	1.24 g
Fiber	0.3 g
Starch	0 g

Protein: 28% 77 kcal
Fat: 69% 187 kcal
Carbohydrates: 3% 8 kcal

CHAPTER-4:
LUNCH CHAFFLES RECIPES

CHICKEN ZINGER CHAFFLE

Prep Time: 15 min
Cooking Time: 15 min
Total Time: 30 min
Servings: 2

INGREDIENTS
- 1 chicken breast, cut into 2 pieces
- 1/2 cup coconut flour
- 1/4 cup finely grated Parmesan
- 1 tsp. paprika
- 1/2 tsp. garlic powder
- 1/2 tsp. onion powder
- 1 tsp. salt& pepper
- 1 egg beaten
- Avocado oil for frying
- Lettuce leaves
- BBQ sauce

CHAFFLE INGREDIENTS
- 4 oz. cheese
- 2 whole eggs
- 2 oz. almond flour
- 1/4 cup almond flour
- 1 tsp baking powder

DIRECTIONS

1. Mix together chaffle ingredients in a bowl.
2. Pour the chaffle batter in preheated greased square chaffle maker.
3. Cook chaffles for about 2-3 minutes until cooked through.
4. Make 4 square chaffles from this batter.
5. Meanwhile mix together coconut flour, parmesan, paprika, garlic powder, onion powder salt and pepper in a bowl.
6. Dip chicken first in coconut flour mixture then in beaten egg.
7. Heat avocado oil in a skillet and cook chicken from both sides. until lightly brown and cooked
8. Set chicken zinger between two chaffles with lettuce and BBQ sauce.
9. Enjoy!

NUTRITIONAL INFORMATION

Amount per serving 288 g

Total Calories	719 kcal
Fats	49.75 g
Protein	53.32 g
Net Carbs	8.1 g
Fiber	6 g
Starch	0.21 g

Protein: 30% 219 kcal
Fat: 60% 435 kcal
Carbohydrates: 9% 66 kcal

CHAFFLE & CHICKEN LUNCH PLATE

Prep Time: 5 min
Cooking Time: 15 min
Total Time: 20 min
Servings: 1

INGREDIENTS
- 1 large egg
- 1/2 cup jack cheese, shredded
- 1 pinch salt

For Serving
- 1 chicken leg
- salt
- pepper
- 1 tsp. garlic, minced
- 1 egg
- I tsp avocado oil

DIRECTIONS
1. Heat your square waffle maker and grease with cooking spray.
2. Pour Chaffle batter intothe skillet and cook for about 2-3 minutes.
3. Meanwhile,heat oil in a pan, over medium heat.
4. Once the oil is hot, add chicken thigh and garlicthen, cook for about 4-5 minutes. Flip and cook for another 3-4 minutes.

5. Season with salt and pepper and give them a good mix.
6. Transfer cooked thigh to plate.
7. Fry the egg in the same pan for about 1-2 minutes according to your choice.
8. Once chaffles are cooked, serve with fried egg and chicken thigh.
9. Enjoy!

NUTRITIONAL INFORMATION

Amount per serving 194 g

Total Calories	440 kcal
Fats	32.92 g
Protein	32.11 g
Net Carbs	1.77 g
Fiber	0.1 g
Starch	0 g

Protein: 31% 138 kcal
Fat: 66% 292 kcal
Carbohydrates: 2% 10 kcal

GRILL PORK CHAFFLE SANDWICH

Prep Time: 5 min
Cooking Time: 15 min
Total Time: 20 min
Servings: 2

INGREDIENTS
*   1/2 cup mozzarella, shredded
*   1 egg
*   I pinch garlic powder

PORK PATTY
*   1/2 cup pork, minced
*   1 tbsp. green onion, diced
*   1/2 tsp Italian seasoning
*   Lettuce leaves

DIRECTIONS
1. Preheat the square waffle maker and grease with
2. Mix together egg, cheese and garlic powder in a small mixing bowl.
3. Pour batter in a preheated waffle maker and close the lid.
4. Make 2 chaffles from thisbatter.
5. Cook chaffles for about 2-3 minutes until cooked through.
6. Meanwhile, mix together pork patty ingredients in a bowl and make 1 large patty.

7. Grill pork patty in a preheated grill for about 3-4 minutes per side until cooked through.
8. Arrange pork patty between two chaffles with lettuce leaves. Cut sandwich to make a triangular sandwich.
9. Enjoy!

NUTRITIONAL INFORMATION

Amount per serving 95 g

Total Calories	181 kcal
Fats	9.58 g
Protein	20.45 g
Net Carbs	1.12 g
Fiber	0.1 g
Starch	0 g

Protein: 48% 85 kcal
Fat: 48% 86 kcal
Carbohydrates: 4% 7 kcal

CRUNCHY FISH AND CHAFFLE BITES

Prep Time: 15 min
Cooking Time: 15 min
Total Time: 20 min
Servings: 4

INGREDIENTS
- 1 lb. cod fillets, sliced into 4 slice
- 1 tsp. sea salt
- 1 tsp. garlic powder
- 1 egg, whisked
- 1 cup almond flour
- 2 tbsp. avocado oil

CHAFFLE INGREDIENTS
- 2 eggs
- 1/2 cup cheddar cheese
- 2 tbsps. almond flour
- ½ tsp. Italian seasoning

DIRECTIONS
1. Mix together chaffle ingredients in a bowl and make 4 square
2. Put the chaffles in a preheated chaffle maker.
3. Mix together the salt, pepper, and garlic powder in a mixing bowl. Toss the cod cubes in this mixture and let sit for 10 minutes.

4. Then dip each cod slice into the egg mixture and then into the almond flour.
5. Heat oil in skillet and fish cubes for about 2-3 minutes, until cooked and browned
6. Serve on chaffles and enjoy!

NUTRITIONAL INFORMATION

Amount per serving 187 g

Total Calories	321 kcal
Fats	21.4 g
Protein	28.74g
Net Carbs	1.27 g
Fiber	1 g
Starch	0.05 g

Protein: 38% 121 kcal
Fat: 59% 189 kcal
Carbohydrates: 3% 11 kcal

DOUBLE CHICKEN CHAFFLES

Prep Time: 5 min
Cooking Time: 5 min
Total Time: 30 min
Servings: 2

INGREDIENTS
- 1/2 cup boil shredded chicken
- 1/4 cup cheddar cheese
- 1/8 cup parmesan cheese
- 1 egg
- 1 tsp. Italian seasoning
- 1/8 tsp. garlic powder
- 1 tsp. cream cheese

DIRECTIONS
1. Preheat the Belgian waffle maker.
2. Mix together in chaffle ingredients in a bowl and mix together.
3. Sprinkle 1 tbsp. of cheese in a waffle maker and pour in chaffle batter.
4. Pour 1 tbsp. of cheese over batter and close the lid.
5. Cook chaffles for about 4 to 5 minutes.
6. Serve with a chicken zinger and enjoy the double chicken flavor.

NUTRITIONAL INFORMATION

Amount per serving 78 g

Total Calories	199 kcal
Fats	14.34 g
Protein	14.35 g
Net Carbs	1.83 g
Fiber	0.2 g
Starch	0 g

Protein: 30% 60 kcal
Fat: 65% 129 kcal
Carbohydrates: 5% 9 kcal

CHICKEN BITES WITH CHAFFLES

Prep Time   5 Min
Cooking Time   10 min
Total Time   15 Min
Servings: 2

INGREDIENTS

- 1 chicken breastscut into 2 x2 inch chunks
- 1 egg, whisked
- 1/4 cup almond flour
- 2 tbsps. onion powder
- 2 tbsps. garlic powder
- 1 tsp. dried oregano
- 1 tsp. paprika powder
- 1 tsp. salt
- 1/2 tsp. black pepper
- 2 tbsps. avocado oil

DIRECTIONS

1. Add all the dry ingredients together into a large bowl. Mix well.
2. Place the eggs into a separate bowl.
3. Dip each chicken piece into the egg and then into the dry ingredients.
4. Heat oil in 10-inch skillet, add oil.
5. Once avocado oil is hot, place the coated chicken nuggets onto a skillet and cook for 6-8 minutes until cooked and golden brown.

6. Serve with chaffles and raspberries.
7. Enjoy!

NUTRITIONAL INFORMATION

Amount per serving 173 g

Total Calories	401 kcal
Fats	28.19 g
Protein	32.35 g
Net Carbs	1.46 g
Fiber	3 g
Starch	0.13 g

CAULIFLOWER CHAFFLES AND TOMATOES

Prep Time: 5 min
Cooking Time: 15 min
Total Time: 20 min
Servings: 2

INGREDIENTS
- 1/2 cup cauliflower
- 1/4 tsp. garlic powder
- 1/4 tsp. black pepper
- 1/4 tsp. Salt
- 1/2 cup shredded cheddar cheese
- 1 egg

FOR TOPPING
- 1 lettuce leave
- 1 tomato sliced
- 4 oz. cauliflower steamed, mashed
- 1 tsp sesame seeds

DIRECTIONS
1. Add all chaffle ingredients into a blender and mix well.
2. Sprinkle 1/8 shredded cheese on the waffle maker and pour cauliflower mixture in a preheated waffle maker and sprinkle the rest of the cheese over it.

3. Cook chaffles for about 4-5 minutes until cooked
4. For serving, lay lettuce leaves over chaffle top with steamed cauliflower and tomato.
5. Drizzle sesame seeds on top.
6. Enjoy!

NUTRITIONAL INFORMATION

Amount per serving 149 g

Total Calories	198 kcal
Fats	14.34 g
Protein	12.74 g
Net Carbs	1.73 g
Fiber	2 g
Starch	0 g

Protein: 25% 49 kcal
Fat: 65% 128 kcal
Carbohydrates: 10% 21 kcal

CHAFFLE WITH CHEESE & BACON

Prep Time: 15 min
Cooking Time: 15 min
Total Time: 30 min
Servings: 2

INGREDIENTS
- 1 egg
- 1/2 cup cheddar cheese, shredded
- 1 tbsp. parmesan cheese
- 3/4 tsp coconut flour
- 1/4 tsp baking powder
- 1/8 tsp Italian Seasoning
- pinch of salt
- 1/4 tsp garlic powder

FOR TOPPING
- 1 bacon sliced, cooked and chopped
- 1/2 cup mozzarella cheese, shredded
- 1/4 tsp parsley, chopped

DIRECTIONS
1. Preheat oven to 400 degrees.
2. Switch on your mini waffle maker and grease with cooking spray.
3. Mix together chaffle ingredients in a mixing bowl until combined.

4. Spoon half of the batter in the center of the waffle maker and close the lid. Cook chaffles for about 3-4 minutes until cooked.
5. Carefully remove chaffles from the maker.
6. Arrange chaffles in a greased baking tray.
7. Top with mozzarella cheese, chopped bacon and parsley.
8. And bake in the oven for 4 -5 minutes.
9. Once the cheese is melted, remove from the oven.
10. Serve and enjoy!

NUTRITIONAL INFORMATION

Amount per serving 107 g

Total Calories	324 kcal
Fats	24.71 g
Protein	22.2 g
Net Carbs	0.95 g
Fiber	0.1 g
Starch	0 g

Protein: 28% 90 kcal
Fat: 69% 222 kcal
Carbohydrates: 3% 11 kcal

CHAFFLE MINI SANDWICH

Prep Time: 5 min
Cooking Time: 10 min
Total Time: 15 min
Servings: 2

INGREDIENTS
- 1 large egg
- 1/8 cup almond flour
- 1/2 tsp. garlic powder
- 3/4 tsp. baking powder
- 1/2 cup shredded cheese

SANDWICH FILLING
- 2 slices deli ham
- 2 slices tomatoes
- 1 slice cheddar cheese

DIRECTIONS
1. Grease your square waffle maker and preheat it on medium heat.
2. Mix together chaffle ingredients in a mixing bowl until well combined.
3. Pour batter intoa square waffle and make two chaffles.
4. Once chaffles are cooked, remove from the maker.
5. For a sandwich,arrange deli ham, tomato slice and cheddar cheese between two chaffles.
6. Cut sandwich from the center.
7. Serve and enjoy!

NUTRITIONAL INFORMATION

Amount per serving 96 g

Total Calories	239 kcal
Fats	17.86 g
Protein	17 g
Net Carbs	0.95 g
Fiber	0.3 g
Starch	0 g

Protein: 29% 70 kcal
Fat: 66% 159 kcal
Carbohydrates: 4% 10 kcal

CHAFFLES WITH TOPPING

Prep Time: 5 min
Cooking Time: 10 min
Total Time: 15 min
Servings: 3

INGREDIENTS
- 1 large egg
- 1 tbsp. almond flour
- 1 tbsp. full-fat Greek yogurt
- 1/8 tsp baking powder
- 1/4 cup shredded Swiss cheese

TOPPING
- 4oz. grillprawns
- 4 oz. steamed cauliflower mash
- 1/2 zucchini sliced
- 3 lettuce leaves
- 1 tomato, sliced
- 1 tbsp. flax seeds

DIRECTIONS
1. Make 3 chaffles with the given chaffles ingredients.
2. For serving, arrange lettuce leaves on each chaffle.
3. Top with zucchini slice, grill prawns, cauliflower mash and a tomato slice.

4. Drizzle flax seeds on top.

5. Serve and enjoy!

NUTRITIONAL INFORMATION

Amount per serving 112 g

Total Calories	158 kcal
Fats	8.41 g
Protein	17.31 g
Net Carbs	1.14 g
Fiber	1.1 g
Starch	0 g

Protein: 45% 71 kcal
Fat: 47% 75 kcal
Carbohydrates: 8% 12 kcal

GRILL BEEFSTEAK AND CHAFFLE

Prep Time: 5 min
Cooking Time: 10 min
Total Time: 15 min
Servings: 1

INGREDIENTS

- 1 beefsteak rib eye
- 1 tsp salt
- 1 tsp pepper
- 1 tbsp. lime juice
- 1 tsp garlic

DIRECTIONS

1. Prepare your grill for direct heat.
2. Mix together all spices and rub over beefsteak evenly.
3. Place the beef on the grill rack over medium heat.
4. Cover and cook steak for about6 to 8 minutes. Flip and cook for another 4-5 minutes until cooked through.
5. Serve with keto simple chaffle and enjoy!

NUTRITIONAL INFORMATION

Amount per serving 177 g

Total Calories	538 kcal
Fats	26.97 g
Protein	68.89 g
Net Carbs	3.07 g
Fiber	0.8 g
Starch	0 g

Protein: 51% 274 kcal

Fat: 45% 243 kcal

Carbohydrates: 4% 22 kcal

CHAFFLE CHEESE SANDWICH

Prep Time: 5 min
Cooking Time: 10 min
Total Time: 15 min
Servings: 1

INGREDIENTS

- 2 square keto chaffle
- 2 slice cheddar cheese
- 2 lettuce leaves

DIRECTIONS

1. Prepare your oven on 400⁰ F.
2. Arrange lettuce leave and cheese slice between chaffles.
3. Bake in the preheated oven for about 4-5 minutes until cheese is melted.
4. Once the cheese is melted, remove from the oven.
5. Serve and enjoy!

NUTRITIONAL INFORMATION

Amount per serving 70 g

Total Calories	215 kcal
Fats	16.69 g
Protein	14.42 g
Net Carbs	1.28 g
Fiber	0.1 g
Starch	0 g

Protein: 28% 60 kcal

Fat: 69% 149 kcal

Carbohydrates: 3% 6 kcal

CHAFFLE EGG SANDWICH

Prep Time: 5 min
Cooking Time: 10 min
Total Time: 15 min
Servings: 2

INGREDIENTS

- 2 MINI keto chaffle
- 2 slice cheddar cheese
- 1 egg simple omelet

DIRECTIONS

1. Prepare your oven on 400⁰ F.
2. Arrange egg omelet and cheese slice between chaffles.
3. Bake in the preheated oven for about 4-5 minutes until cheese is melted.
4. Once the cheese is melted, remove from the oven.
5. Serve and enjoy!

NUTRITIONAL INFORMATION

Amount per serving 185 g

Total Calories	495 kcal
Fats	37.65 g
Protein	34.41 g
Net Carbs	2.59 g
Fiber	0.2 g
Starch	0.01 g

Protein: 29% 144 kcal
Fat: 68% 337 kcal
Carbohydrates: 3% 14 kcal

CHAPTER-5:
AFTERNOON SNACKS RECIPES

LETTUCE CHAFFLE SANDWICH

Prep Time: 5 min
Cooking Time: 5 min
Total Time: 10 min
Servings: 2

INGREDIENTS
- 1 large egg
- 1 tbsp. almond flour
- 1 tbsp. full-fat Greek yogurt
- 1/8 tsp baking powder
- 1/4 cup shredded Swiss cheese
- 4 lettuce leaves

DIRECTIONS
1. Switch on your mini waffle maker.
2. Grease it with cooking spray.
3. Mix together egg, almond flour, yogurts, baking powder and cheese in mixing bowl.
4. Pour 1/2 cup of the batter into the center of your waffle iron and close the lid.
5. Cook chaffles for about 2-3 minutes untilcooked through.
6. Repeat with remaining batter
7. Once cooked, carefully transfer to plate. Serve lettuce leaves between 2 chaffles.
8. Enjoy!

NUTRITIONAL INFORMATION

Amount per serving 54 g

Total Calories	183 kcal
Fats	13.97 g
Protein	10.08 g
Net Carbs	1.81 g
Fiber	1.8 g
Starch	0.1 g

Protein: 22% 40 kcal
Fat: 66% 120 kcal
Carbohydrates: 12% 22 kcal

AVOCADO CHAFFLES

Prep Time: 5 min
Cooking Time: 5 min
Total Time: 10 min
Servings: 2

INGREDIENTS
- 1 large egg
- 1/2 cup finely shredded mozzarella
- 1/8 cup avocado mash
- 1 tbsp. coconut cream

TOPPING
- 2 oz. smoked salmon
- 1 Avocado thinly sliced

DIRECTIONS
1. Switch on your square waffle maker and grease with cooking spray.
2. Beat egg in a mixing bowl with a fork.
3. Add the cheese, avocado mash and coconut cream to the egg and mix well.
4. Pour chaffle mixture in thepreheated waffle maker and cook for about 2-3 minutes.
5. Once chaffles are cooked, carefully remove from the maker.
6. Serve with an avocado slice and smoked salmon.
7. Drizzle ground pepper on top.

8. Enjoy!

NUTRITIONAL INFORMATION

Amount per serving 214 g

Total Calories	399 kcal
Fats	30.02 g
Protein	22.08 g
Net Carbs	2.37 g
Fiber	7.6 g
Starch	0.12 g

Protein: 23% 90 kcal
Fat: 67% 266 kcal
Carbohydrates: 11% 42 kcal

SIMPLE HEART SHAPE CHAFFLES

Prep Time: 5 min
Cooking Time: 5 min
Total Time: 10 min
Servings: 4

INGREDIENTS
- 2 large eggs
- 1 cup finely shredded mozzarella
- 2 tbsps. coconut flour
- 1 tsp. stevia
- Coconut flour for topping

DIRECTIONS
1. Switch on your heart shape Belgian waffle maker.
2. Grease with cooking spray and let it preheat.
3. Mix together chaffle ingredients in a mixing bowl.
4. Pour chaffle mixture in heart shape Belgian makerand cook for about 4-5 minutes.
5. Once chaffles are cooked, carefully remove from the maker.
6. Sprinkle coconut flour on top.
7. Serve with warm keto BLT coffee.
8. Enjoy!

NUTRITIONAL INFORMATION

Amount per serving 117 g

Total Calories	163 kcal
Fats	10.5 g
Protein	12.82g
Net Carbs	0.71 g
Fiber	1.2 g
Starch	0 g

Protein: 32% 52 kcal
Fat: 57% 93 kcal
Carbohydrates: 10% 17 kcal

COCOA CHAFFLES WITH COCONUT CREAM

Prep Time: 5 min
Total Time: 5 min
Servings: 2

INGREDIENTS
- 1 egg
- 1/2 cup mozzarella cheese
- 1 tsp stevia
- 1 tsp vanilla
- 2 tbsps. almond flour
- 1 tbsp. sugar-free chocolate chips
- 2 tbsps. cocoa powder

TOPPING
- 1 scoop coconut cream
- 1 tbsp. coconut flour

DIRECTIONS
1. Mix together chaffle ingredients in a bowl and mix well.
2. Preheat your dash mini waffle maker. Spray waffle maker with cooking spray.
3. Pour 1/2 batter into the mini-waffle maker and close the lid.
4. Cook chaffles for about 2-4 minutes and remove from the maker.
5. Make chaffles from the rest of the batter.

6. Serve with a scoop of coconut cream between two chaffles.
7. Drizzle coconut flour on top.
8. Enjoy with afternoon coffee!

NUTRITIONAL INFORMATION

Amount per serving 79 g

Total Calories	239 kcal
Fats	17.59 g
Protein	15.13 g
Net Carbs	1.68 g
Fiber	2 g
Starch	0.1 g

Protein: 26% 60 kcal
Fat: 65% 152 kcal
Carbohydrates: 9% 21 kcal

CHAFFLE WITH CREAM AND SALMON

Prep Time: 10 min
Cooking Time: 20 min
Total Time: 30 min
Servings: 4

INGREDIENTS

- 1/2 medium onion sliced
- 2 tbsps. parsley chopped
- 4 oz. smoked salmon
- 4 tbsp. heavy cream

CHAFFLE INGREDIENTS

- 1 egg
- 1/2 cup mozzarella cheese
- 1 tsp stevia
- 1 tsp vanilla
- 2 tbsps. almond flour

DIRECTIONS

1. Make 4 Heart shape chaffles with the chaffle ingredients
2. Arrange smoked salmon and heavy cream on each Chaffle.
3. Top with onion slice and parsley.

4. Serve as it is and enjoy!

NUTRITIONAL INFORMATION

Amount per serving 132 g

Total Calories	231 kcal
Fats	15.4 g
Protein	19.47 g
Net Carbs	1.41 g
Fiber	1 g
Starch	0 g

Protein: 34% 79 kcal
Fat: 60% 137 kcal
Carbohydrates: 6% 14 kcal

MIDDAY CHAFFLE SNACKS

Prep Time: 5 min
Cooking Time: 5 min
Total Time: 55 min
Servings: 4

INGREDIENTS
- 4 Mini Chaffles
- 2 oz. coconut flakes
- 2 oz. kiwi slice
- 2 oz. raspberry
- 2 oz. almonds chopped

CHAFFLE INGREDIENTS

- 1 egg
- 1/2 cup mozzarella cheese
- 1 tsp stevia
- 1 tsp vanilla
- 2 tbsps. almond flour

DIRECTIONS
1. Make 4 mini chaffles with the chaffle ingredients.
2. Arrange coconut flakes, raspberries, almonds and raspberries on each chaffle.
3. Serve and enjoy keto snacks

NUTRITIONAL INFORMATION

Amount per serving 72 g

Total Calories	208 kcal
Fats	16.08 g
Protein	9.69 g
Net Carbs	1.23 g
Fiber	4 g
Starch	0.11 g

Protein: 18% 37 kcal
Fat: 67% 137 kcal
Carbohydrates: 15% 31 kc

CHAFFLES WITH CHOCOLATE BALLS

Prep Time: 5 min
Total Time: 5 min
Servings: 2

INGREDIENTS
- 1/4 cup heavy cream
- ½ cup unsweetened cocoa powder
- 1/4 cup coconut meat

CHAFFLE INGREDIENTS
- 1 egg
- ½ cup mozzarella cheese

DIRECTIONS
1. Make 2 chaffles with chaffle ingredients.
2. Meanwhile, mix together all ingredients in a mixing bowl.
3. Make two balls from the mixture and freeze in the freezer for about 2 hours until set.
4. Serve with keto chaffles and enjoy!

NUTRITIONAL INFORMATION

Amount per serving 80 g

Total Calories	253 kcal
Fats	22.15 g
Protein	11.34 g
Net Carbs	0.42 g
Fiber	0.9 g
Starch	0 g

Protein: 18% 46 kcal
Fat: 78% 196 kcal
Carbohydrates: 4% 10 kcal

CHAFFLE AND CHEESE SANDWICH

Prep Time   5 Min
Cooking Time   5 min
Total Time   10 Min
Servings: 3

INGREDIENTS

- 1 egg
- ½ cup mozzarella cheese
- 1 tsp. baking powder
- 3 slice feta cheese for topping

DIRECTIONS

1. Make 6 mini chaffles
2. Set feta cheese between two chaffles.
3. Serve with hot coffee and enjoy!

NUTRITIONAL INFORMATION

Amount per serving 72 g

Total Calories	183 kcal
Fats	12.38 g
Protein	13.47 g
Net Carbs	1.73 g
Fiber	0 g
Starch	0 g

Protein: 31% 56 kcal
Fat: 60% 110 kcal
Carbohydrates: 9% 16 kcal

CHAPTER-6:
CHAFFLE DESSERT RECIPES

CHAFFLE STRAWBERY SANDWICH

Prep Time: 5 min
Total Time: 5 min
Servings: 2

INGREDIENTS
- 1/4 cup heavy cream
- 4 oz. strawberry slice

CHAFFLE INGREDIENTS
- 1 egg
- ½ cup mozzarella cheese

DIRECTIONS
1. Make 2 chaffles with chaffle ingredients
2. Meanwhile, mix together cream and strawberries.
3. Spread this mixture over chaffle slice.
4. Drizzle chocolate sauce over a sandwich.
5. Serve and enjoy!

NUTRITIONAL INFORMATION

Amount per serving 80 g

Total Calories	253 kcal
Fats	22.15 g
Protein	11.34 g
Net Carbs	0.42 g
Fiber	0.9 g
Starch	0 g

Protein: 18% 46 kcal
Fat: 78% 196 kcal
Carbohydrates: 4% 10 kcal

CRUNCHY COCONUT CHAFFLES CAKE

Prep Time: 5 min
Cooking Time: 15 min
Total Time: 20 min
Servings: 4

INGREDIENTS
- 4 large eggs
- 1 cup shredded cheese
- 2 tbsps. coconut cream
- 2 tbsps. coconut flour.
- 1 tsp. stevia

TOPPING
- 1 cup heavy cream
- 8 oz. raspberries
- 4 oz. blueberries
- 2 oz. cherries

DIRECTIONS
1. Make 4 thin round chaffles with the chaffle ingredients. Once chaffles are cooked, set in layers ona plate.
2. Spread heavy cream in each layer.
3. Top with raspberries then blueberries and cherries.

4. Serve and enjoy!

NUTRITIONAL INFORMATION

Amount per serving 216 g

Total Calories	318 kcal
Fats	26.05 g
Protein	15.72 g
Net Carbs	0.26 g
Fiber	1.1 g
Starch	0 g

Protein: 21% 67 kcal
Fat: 72% 230 kcal
Carbohydrates: 7% 21 kcal

DOUBLE DECKER CHAFFLE

Prep Time: 5 min
Cooking Time: 10 min
Total Time: 15 min
Servings: 2

INGREDIENTS
- 1 large egg
- 1 cup shredded cheese

TOPPING
- 1 keto chocolate ball
- 2 oz. cranberries
- 2 oz. blueberries
- 4 oz. cranberries puree

DIRECTIONS
1. Make 2 mini dash waffles.
2. Put cranberries and blueberries in the freezer for about 2 hours.
3. For serving, arrange keto chocolate ball between 2 chaffles.
4. Top with frozen berries,
5. Serve and enjoy!

NUTRITIONAL INFORMATION

Amount per serving 148 g

Total Calories	333 kcal
Fats	24.83 g
Protein	19.33 g
Net Carbs	2.37 g
Fiber	2 g
Starch	0.01 g

Protein: 23% 78 kcal
Fat: 67% 223 kcal
Carbohydrates: 9% 31 kcal

YOGURT CHAFFLE

Prep Time: 5 min
Cooking Time: 10 min
Total Time: 15 min
Servings: 4

INGREDIENTS
- 1/2 cup mozzarella cheese, shredded
- 1/2 cup cheddar cheese, shredded
- 1 egg
- 2 tbsps. ground almonds
- 1 tsp. psyllium husk
- ¼ tsp. baking powder
- 1 tbsp. Greek yogurt

TOPPING
- 1 scoop heavy cream, frozen
- 1 scoop raspberry puree, frozen
- 2 raspberries

DIRECTIONS
1. Mix together all of the chaffle ingredients and heat up your Waffle Maker.
2. Let thebatter stand for 5 minutes.
3. Spray waffles maker with cooking spray.

4. spread some cheese on chaffle maker and pour chaffle mixture in heart shape Belgian waffle maker.
5. Close the lid and cook for about 4-5 minutes.
6. For serving, scoop frozen cream and puree in the middle of chaffle.
7. Top with a raspberry.
8. Serve and enjoy!

NUTRITIONAL INFORMATION

Amount per serving 45 g

Total Calories	133 kcal
Fats	9.75 g
Protein	10.02 g
Net Carbs	1.59 g
Fiber	0.1 g
Starch	0 g

Protein: 31% 41 kcal
Fat: 66% 88 kcal
Carbohydrates: 3% 4 kcal

KETO CHAFFLE WITH ICE-CREAM

Prep Time: 5 min
Cooking Time: 5 min
Total Time: 10 min
Servings: 2

INGREDIENTS

- 1 egg
- 1/2 cup cheddar cheese, shredded
- 1 tbsp. almond flour
- ½ tsp. baking powder.

FOR SERVING

- 1/2 cup heavy cream
- 1 tbsp. keto chocolate chips.
- 2 oz. raspberries
- 2 oz. blueberries

DIRECTIONS

1. Preheat your mini waffle maker according to the manufacturer's instructions.
2. Mix together chaffle ingredients in a small bowl and make 2 mini chaffles.

3. For an ice-cream ball, mix cream and chocolate chips in a bowl and pour this mixture in 2 silicone molds.
4. Freeze the ice-cream balls in a freezer for about 2-4 hours.
5. For serving, set ice-cream ball on chaffle.
6. Top with berries and enjoy!

NUTRITIONAL INFORMATION

Amount per serving 87 g

Total Calories	273 kcal
Fats	24.61 g
Protein	11.42 g
Net Carbs	1 g
Fiber	0.1 g
Starch	0 g

Protein: 17% 47 kcal
Fat: 80% 219 kcal
Carbohydrates: 3% 7 kcal

WALNUTS LOWCARB CHAFFLES

Prep Time   5 Min
Cooking Time   5 min
Total Time   10Min
Servings: 2

INGREDIENTS

- 2 tbsps. cream cheese
- ½ tsp almonds flour
- ¼ tsp. baking powder
- 1 large egg
- ¼ cup chopped walnuts
- Pinch of stevia extract powder

DIRECTIONS

1. Preheat your waffle maker.
2. Spray waffle maker with cooking spray.
3. In a bowl, add cream cheese, almond flour, baking powder, egg, walnuts, and stevia.
4. Mix all ingredients,
5. Spoon walnut batter in the waffle maker and cook for about 2-3 minutes.
6. Let chaffles cool at room temperature before serving.

NUTRITIONAL INFORMATION

Amount per serving 19 g

Total Calories	95 kcal
Fats	8.93 g
Protein	2.94 g
Net Carbs	1.03 g
Fiber	0.7 g
Starch	0.01 g

Protein: 12% 11 kcal
Fat: 80% 76 kcal
Carbohydrates: 8% 8 kcal

CREAMY CHAFFLES

Prep Time   5 Min
Cooking Time   5 min
Total Time   10 Min
Servings: 4

INGREDIENTS
- 1 cup egg whites
- 1 cup cheddar cheese, shredded
- 2 oz. cocoa powder.
- 1 pinch salt

TOPPING
- 4 oz. cream cheese
- Strawberries
- Blueberries
- Coconut flour

DIRECTIONS
1. Beat eggs whites with beater until fluffy and white
2. Chop Italian cheese with a knife and beat with egg whites.
3. Add cocoa powder and salt in mixture and again beat.
4. Spray round waffle maker non-stick cooking spray.

5. Pour batter in a round waffle maker.
6. Cook the chaffle for about 5 minutes.
7. Once cooked carefully remove chaffle from the maker.
8. For serving, spread cream cheese on chaffle. Top with strawberries, blueberries and coconut flour.
9. Serve and enjoy!

NUTRITIONAL INFORMATION

Amount per serving 125 g

Total Calories	263 kcal
Fats	20.98 g
Protein	16.26 g
Net Carbs	0.59 g
Fiber	0.1 g
Starch	0.1 g

Protein: 26% 68 kcal
Fat: 71% 187 kcal
Carbohydrates: 3% 9 kcal

CHAFFLES ICECREAM TOPPING

Prep Time: 5 min
Total Time: 5 min
Servings: 2

INGREDIENTS
- 1/4 cup coconut cream, frozen
- 1 cup coconut flour
- ¼ cup strawberries chunks
- 1 tsp. vanilla extract
- 1 oz. chocolate flakes
- 4 keto chaffles

DIRECTIONS
1. Mix together all ingredients in a mixing bowl.
2. Spread mixture between 2 chaffles and freeze in the freezer for 2 hours.
3. Serve chill and enjoy!

NUTRITIONAL INFORMATION

Amount per serving 125 g

Total Calories	263 kcal
Fats	20.98 g
Protein	16.26 g
Net Carbs	0.59 g
Fiber	0.1 g
Starch	0.1 g

Protein: 26% 68 kcal
Fat: 71% 187 kcal
Carbohydrates: 3% 9 kcal

CHAFFLES WITH STRAWBERRY FROSTY

Prep Time: 5 min
Total Time: 5 min
Servings: 2

INGREDIENTS
- 1 cup frozen strawberries
- 1/2 cup Heavy cream
- 1 tsp stevia
- 1 scoop protein powder
- 3 keto chaffles

DIRECTIONS
1. Mix together all ingredients in a mixing bowl.
2. Pour mixture in silicone molds and freeze in a freezer for about 4 hours to set.
3. Once frosty is set, top on keto chaffles and enjoy!

NUTRITIONAL INFORMATION

Amount per serving 141 g

Total Calories	142 kcal
Fats	11.22 g
Protein	1.09 g
Net Carbs	0.95 g
Fiber	0.4 g
Starch	0 g

Protein: 13% 40 kcal
Fat: 69% 99 kcal
Carbohydrates: 18% 10 kcal

CHOCOLATE CHAFFLE ROLLS

Prep Time: 5 min
Cooking Time 10 min
Total Time: 15 min
Servings: 2

INGREDIENTS
- 1/2 cup mozzarella cheese
- 1 tbsp. almond flour
- 1 egg
- 1 tsp cinnamon
- 1 tsp stevia

FILLING
- 1 tbsp. coconut cream
- 1 tbsp. coconut flour
- 1/4 cup keto chocolate chips

DIRECTIONS
1. Switch on a round waffle maker and let it heat up.
2. In a small bowl, mix together cheese, egg, flour, cinnamon powder, and stevia in a bowl.
3. Spray the round waffle maker with nonstick spray.
4. Pour the batter in a waffle maker and close the lid.
5. Close the waffle maker and cook for about 3-4 minutes.

6. Once chaffles are cooked remove from Maker
7. Meanwhile, mix together cream flour and chocolate chips in bowl and microwave for 30 sec.
8. Spread this filling over chaffle and roll it.
9. Serve and enjoy!

NUTRITIONAL INFORMATION

Amount per serving 72 g

Total Calories	156 kcal
Fats	10.62 g
Protein	12.32 g
Net Carbs	1.38 g
Fiber	1 g
Starch	0 g

Protein: 32% 50 kcal
Fat: 61% 94 kcal

Carbohydrates: 7% 11 kcal

CINNAMON CHAFFLE ROLLS

Prep Time: 5 min
Cooking Time 10 min
Total Time: 15 min
Servings: 2

INGREDIENTS
- 1/2 cup mozzarella cheese
- 1 tbsp. almond flour
- 1 egg
- 1 tsp cinnamon
- 1 tsp stevia

CINNAMON ROLL GLAZE
- 1 tbsp. butter
- 1 tbsp. cream cheese
- 1 tsp. cinnamon
- 1/4 tsp vanilla extract
- 1 tbsp. coconut flour

DIRECTIONS
- Switch on a round waffle maker and let it heat up.
- In a small bowl mix together cheese, egg, flour, cinnamon powder, and stevia in a bowl.
- Spray the roundwaffle maker with nonstick spray.

- Pour the batter in a waffle maker and close the lid.
- Close the waffle maker and cook for about 3-4 minutes.
- Once chaffles are cooked, remove from Maker
- Mix together butter, cream cheese, cinnamon, vanilla and coconut flour in a bowl.
- Spread this glaze over chaffle and roll up.
- Serve and enjoy!

NUTRITIONAL INFORMATION

Amount per serving 81 g

Total Calories	210 kcal
Fats	15.99 g
Protein	12.72 g
Net Carbs	1.42 g
Fiber	1.5 g
Starch	0 g

Protein: 25% 52 kcal
Fat: 69% 142 kcal
Carbohydrates: 7% 14 kcal

CHAPTER-7:
BROWNIES CHAFFLE RECIPES

BEGINNER BROWNIES CHAFFLE

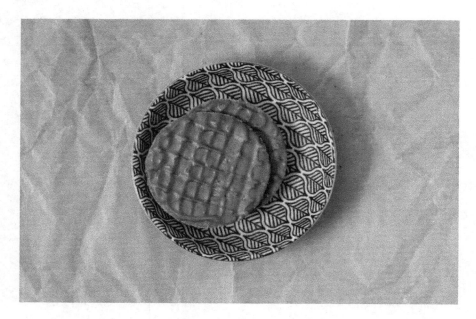

Prep Time   5 min
Cooking Time   5 min
Total Time   10 Min
Servings: 2

INGREDIENTS
- 1 cup cheddar cheese
- 1 tbsp. cocoa powder
- ½ tsp baking powder
- 1 large egg.
- ¼ cup melted keto chocolate chips for topping

DIRECTIONS
1. Preheat dash mini waffle iron and grease it.
2. Blend all ingredients in a blender until mixed.
3. Pour 1 tsp. cheese in a waffle maker and then pour the mixture in the center of greased waffle.
4. Again sprinkle cheese on the batter.
5. Close the waffle maker.
6. Cook chaffles for about 4-5 minutes until cooked and crispy.
7. Once chaffles are cooked remove.
8. Top with melted chocolate and enjoy!

NUTRITIONAL INFORMATION

Amount per serving 99 g

Total Calories	332 kcal
Fats	26.57 g
Protein	19.77 g
Net Carbs	2.47 g
Fiber	1.2 g
Starch	0 g

Protein: 24% 79 kcal
Fat: 72% 239 kcal
Carbohydrates: 4% 14 kcal

CHOCOLATE BROWNIE CHAFFLES

Prep Time   5 Min
Cooking Time   5 min
Total Time   10 Min
Servings: 2

INGREDIENTS
- 2 tbsp. cocoa powder
- 1 egg
- 1/4 tsp baking powder
- 1 tbsp. heavy whipping cream
- ½ cup mozzarella cheese

DIRECTIONS
1. Beat egg with a fork in a small mixing bowl.
2. Add the remaining ingredients in a beaten eggand beat well with a beater until the mixture is smooth and fluffy.
3. Pour batter in a greased preheated waffle maker.
4. Close the lid.
5. Cook chaffles for about 4 minutes until they are thoroughlycooked.
6. Serve with berries and enjoy!

NUTRITIONAL INFORMATION

Amount per serving 69 g

Total Calories	162 kcal
Fats	11.22 g
Protein	12.97 g
Net Carbs	2.45 g
Fiber	1.6 g
Starch	0 g

Protein: 32% 51 kcal
Fat: 62% 100 kcal
Carbohydrates: 6% 10 kcal

SUPER EASY CHOCOLATE CHAFFLES

Prep Time   5 Min
Cooking Time   5 min
Total Time   10 Min
Servings: 2

INGREDIENTS

- 1/4 cup unsweetened chocolate chips
- 1 egg
- 2 tbsps. almond flour
- 1/2 cup mozzarella cheese
- 1 tbsp. Greek yogurts
- 1/2 tsp. baking powder
- 1 tsp. stevia

DIRECTIONS

1. Switch on your square chaffle maker.
2. Spray the waffle maker with cooking spray.
3. Mix together all recipe ingredients in a mixing bowl.
4. Spoon batter in a greased waffle maker and make two chaffles.
5. Once chaffles are cooked, remove from the maker.
6. Serve with coconut cream, shredded chocolate, and nuts on top.
7. Enjoy!

NUTRITIONAL INFORMATION

Amount per serving 78 g

Total Calories	170 kcal
Fats	11.08 g
Protein	14.25 g
Net Carbs	1.39 g
Fiber	0.2 g
Starch	0.01 g

Protein: 35% 59 kcal
Fat: 59% 99 kcal
Carbohydrates: 6% 10 kcal

DOUBLE CHOCOLATE CHAFFLES

Prep Time   5 Min
Cooking Time   5 min
Total Time   10 Min
Servings: 2

INGREDIENTS

- 1/4 cup unsweetened chocolate chips
- 2 tbsps. cocoa powder
- 1 cup egg whites
- 1 tsp. coffee powder
- 2 tbsps. almond flour
- 1/2 cup mozzarella cheese
- 1 tbsp. coconut milk
- 1 tsp. baking powder
- 1 tsp. stevia

DIRECTIONS

1. Switch on your Belgian chaffle maker.
2. Spray the waffle maker with cooking spray.
3. Beat egg whites with an electric beater until fluffy and white.
4. Add the rest of the ingredients tothe egg whites and mix them again.
5. Pour batter in a greased waffle maker and make two fluffy chaffles.
6. Once chaffles are cooked, remove from the maker.
7. Serve with coconut cream, and berries

8. Enjoy!

NUTRITIONAL INFORMATION

Amount per serving 167 g

Total Calories	188 kcal
Fats	8.28 g
Protein	22.84 g
Net Carbs	2.59 g
Fiber	0.7 g
Starch	0.01 g

Protein: 52% 96 kcal
Fat: 39% 73 kcal
Carbohydrates: 9% 17 kcal

OREO COOKIES CHAFFLES

Prep Time   5 Min
Cooking Time   5 min
Total Time   10 Min
Servings: 3

INGREDIENTS
- 1 egg
- 2 tbsps. almond flour
- 1 tbsp. peanut butter
- 1/2 tsp. baking powder
- 1 tsp. stevia
- 2 tbsps. cream cheese
- 2 tbsps. black cocoa powder
- 1 tbsp. mayonnaise
- 2 tbsps. chocolate chips

DIRECTIONS
1. In a small bowl, beat an egg with an electric beater.
2. Add the remaining ingredients and mix well until the batter is smooth and fluffy.
3. Divide the batter into 3 portions.
4. Pour the batter in a mini round greased waffle maker.

5. Cook Oreo chaffle cookies for about 2-3 minutes until cooked.
6. Drizzle coconut flour on top.
7. Serve and enjoy!

NUTRITIONAL INFORMATION

Amount per serving 46 g

Total Calories	134 kcal
Fats	10.66 g
Protein	7.18 g
Net Carbs	0.88 g
Fiber	0.3 g
Starch	0.01 g

Protein: 22% 29 kcal
Fat: 72% 96 kcal
Carbohydrates: 7% 9 kcal

CHOCO AND STRAWBERRIES CHAFFLES

Prep Time   5 Min
Cooking Time 5 min
Total Time   10 Min
Servings: 2

INGREDIENTS

- 1 tbsp. almond flour
- 1/2 cup strawberry puree
- 1/2 cup cheddar cheese
- 1 tbsp. cocoa powder
- ½ tsp baking powder
- 1 large egg.
- 2 tbsps. coconut oil. melted
- 1/2 tsp vanilla extract optional

DIRECTIONS

1. Preheat waffle iron while you are mixing the ingredients.
2. Melt oil in a microwave.
3. In a small mixing bowl, mix together flour, baking powder, flour, and vanilla until well combined.
4. Add egg, melted oil, ½ cup cheese and strawberry puree tothe flour mixture.
5. Pour 1/8 cup cheese in a waffle maker and then pour the mixture in the center of greased waffle.
6. Again sprinkle cheese on the batter.
7. Close the waffle maker.

8. Cook chaffles for about 4-5 minutes until cooked and crispy.
9. Once chaffles are cooked,remove and enjoy!

NUTRITIONAL INFORMATION

Amount per serving 113 g

Total Calories	312 kcal
Fats	27.91 g
Protein	11.93 g
Net Carbs	2.06 g
Fiber	1.6 g
Starch	0.02 g

Protein: 15% 48 kcal
Fat: 79% 246 kcal
Carbohydrates: 5% 17 kcal

CHOCO AND SPINACH CHAFFLES

Prep Time   5 Min
Cooking Time   5 min
Total Time   10 Min
Servings: 2

INGREDIENTS
- 1 tbsp. almond flour
- ½ cup chopped spinach
- 1/2 cup cheddar cheese
- 1 tbsp. cocoa powder
- ½ tsp baking powder
- 1 large egg.
- 2 tbsps. almond butter
- 1/2 tsp salt
- 1/2 tsp pepper

DIRECTIONS
1. Preheat waffle iron while you are mixing the ingredients.
2. Blend all ingredients in a blender until mixed.
3. Pour 1/8 cup cheese in a waffle maker and then pour the mixture in the center of greased waffle.
4. Again sprinkle cheese on the batter.
5. Close the waffle maker.
6. Cook chaffles for about 4-5 minutes until cooked and crispy.
7. Once chaffles are cooked remove and enjoy.

NUTRITIONAL INFORMATION

Amount per serving 83 g

Total Calories	187 kcal
Fats	14.25 g
Protein	12.13 g
Net Carbs	2.19 g
Fiber	1.2 g
Starch	0 g

Protein: 26% 48 kcal
Fat: 68% 128 kcal
Carbohydrates: 6% 11 kcal

CHAFFLES AND ICE-CREAM PLATTER

Prep Time   5 min
Cooking Time   5 min
Total Time   10 Min
Servings: 2

INGREDIENTS
- 2 keto brownie chaffles
- 2 scoop vanilla keto ice cream
- 8 oz. strawberries, sliced
- keto chocolate sauce

DIRECTIONS
1. Arrange chaffles, ice-cream, strawberries slice in serving plate.
2. Drizzle chocolate sauce on top.
3. Serve and enjoy!

NUTRITIONAL INFORMATION

Amount per serving 83 g

Total Calories	187 kcal
Fats	14.25 g
Protein	12.13 g
Net Carbs	2.19 g
Fiber	1.2 g
Starch	0 g

Protein: 26% 48 kcal
Fat: 68% 128 kcal
Carbohydrates: 6% 11 kcal

KETO COFFEE CHAFFLES

Prep Time   5 Min
Cooking Time 5 min
Total Time   10 Min
Servings: 2

INGREDIENTS
- 1 tbsp. almond flour
- 1 tbsp. instant coffee
- 1/2 cup cheddar cheese
- ½ tsp baking powder
- 1 large egg

DIRECTIONS
1. Preheat waffle iron and grease with cooking spray
2. Meanwhile, in a small mixing bowl, mix together all ingredients and ½ cup cheese.

3. Pour 1/8 cup cheese in a waffle maker and then pour the mixture in the center of greased waffle.
4. Again, sprinkle cheese on the batter.
5. Close the waffle maker.
6. Cook chaffles for about 4-5 minutes until cooked and crispy.
7. Once chaffles are cooked, remove and enjoy!

NUTRITIONAL INFORMATION

Amount per serving 61 g

Total Calories	180 kcal
Fats	13.85 g
Protein	11.38 g
Net Carbs	2.16 g
Fiber	0.1 g
Starch	0 g

Protein: 26% 47 kcal
Fat: 69% 125 kcal
Carbohydrates: 5% 9 kcal

CINNAMON ROLL CHAFFLES

Prep Time   5 Min
Cooking Time 5 min
Total Time   10 Min
Servings: 2

INGREDIENTS
- 1 tbsp. almond flour
- 1 tsp. cinnamon powder
- 1/2 cup cheddar cheese
- 1 tbsp. cocoa powder
- ½ tsp baking powder
- 1 large egg.
- 2 tbsps. peanut oil for topping

DIRECTIONS
1. Preheat waffle maker and mix together all ingredients in a bowl.
2. Pour the chaffle mixture in the center of the greased waffle maker.
3. Close the waffle maker.
4. Cook chaffles for about 4-5 minutes until cooked and crispy.
5. Once chaffles are cooked, remove.
6. Pour melted butter oil on top.
7. Serve and enjoy!

NUTRITIONAL INFORMATION

Amount per serving 77 g

Total Calories	303 kcal
Fats	27.71 g
Protein	11.74 g
Net Carbs	2.07 g
Fiber	1.6 g
Starch	0 g

Protein: 15% 47 kcal

Fat: 81% 247 kcal

Carbohydrates: 3% 9 kcal

CHAPTER-8:
FESTIVE CHAFFLE RECIPES

NEW YEAR KETO CHAFFLE CAKE

Prep Time   5 min
Cooking time   15min
Total time   20 min
Servings   5

INGREDIENTS
- 4 oz. almond flour
- 2 cup cheddar cheese
- 5 eggs
- 1 tsp. stevia
- 2 tsp baking powder
- 2 tsp vanilla extract
- 1/4 cup almond butter, melted
- 3 tbsps. almond milk
- 1 cup cranberries
- I cup coconut cream

DIRECTIONS
1. Crack eggs in a small mixing bowl, mix the eggs, almond flour, stevia, and baking powder.
2. Add the melted butter slowly to the flour mixture, mix well to ensure a smooth consistency.

3. Add the cheese, almond milk, cranberries and vanilla to the flour and butter mixture be sure to mix well.
4. Preheat waffles maker according to manufacturer instruction and grease it with avocado oil.
5. Pour mixture into waffle maker and cook until golden brown.
6. Make 5 chaffles
7. Stag chaffles in a plate. Spread the cream all around.
8. Cut in slice and serve.

NUTRITIONAL INFORMATION

Amount per serving 112 g

Total Calories	243kcal
Fats	42.44.72 g
Protein	7.87g
Net Carbs	1.67 g
Fiber	0 g
Starch	0 g

Protein: 3% 15 Kcal
Fat: 94% 207 Kcal
Carbohydrates: 3% 15 Kcal

THANKSGIVING KETO CHAFFLES

Prep Time   5 min
Cooking time   15min
Total time   20 min
Servings   5

INGREDIENTS
- 4 oz. cheese, shredded
- 5 eggs
- 1 tsp. stevia
- 1 tsp baking powder
- 2 tsp vanilla extract
- 1/4 cup almond butter, melted
- 3 tbsps. almond milk
- 1 tsp avocado oil for greasing

DIRECTIONS
1. Crack eggs in a small mixing bowl; mix the eggs, almond flour, stevia, and baking powder.
2. Add the melted butter slowly to the flour mixture, mix well to ensure a smooth consistency.
3. Add the almond milk and vanilla to the flour and butter mixture, be sure to mix well.

4. Preheat waffles maker according to the manufacturer's instruction and grease it with avocado oil.
5. Pour the mixture into the waffle maker and cook until golden brown.
6. Dust coconut flour on chaffles and serve with coconut cream on the top.

NUTRITIONAL INFORMATION

Amount per serving 112 g

Total Calories	243 kcal
Fats	42.44 g
Protein	7.87 g
Net Carbs	1.67 g
Fiber	0.2g
Starch	0 g

Protein: 3% 15 Kcal
Fat: 94% 207 Kcal
Carbohydrates: 3% 15 Kcal

NEW YEAR CINNAMON CHAFFLE WITH COCONUT CREAM

Prep Time   5 min
Cooking time   5min
Total time   10 min
Servings   2

INGREDIENTS
- 2 large eggs
- 1/8 cup almond flour
- 1 tsp. cinnamon powder
- 1 tsp. sea salt
- 1/2 tsp. baking soda
- 1 cup shredded mozzarella

FOR TOPPING
- 2 tbsps. coconut cream
- 1 tbsp. unsweetened chocolate sauce

DIRECTIONS
1. Preheat waffle maker according to the manufacturer's directions.
2. Mix together recipe ingredients in a mixing bowl.
3. Add cheese and mix well.

4. Pour about ½ cup mixture into the center of the waffle maker and cook for about 2-3 minutes until golden and crispy.
5. Repeat with the remaining batter.
6. For serving, coat coconut cream over chaffles. Drizzle chocolate sauce over chaffle.
7. Freeze chaffle in the freezer for about10 minutes.
8. Serve on Christmas morning and enjoy!

NUTRITIONAL INFORMATION

Amount per serving 122 g

Total Calories	26o kcal
Fats	16.11 g
Protein	24.5 g
Net Carbs	2.38 g
Fiber	0.7 g
Starch	0 g

Protein: 39% 100 kcal
Fat: 56% 145 kcal
Carbohydrates: 5% 13 kcal

CHRISTMAS SMOOTHIE
WITH CHAFFLES

Prep Time   5 min
Cooking time   0 min
Total time   5 min
Servings   2

INGREDIENTS
- 1 cupcoconutmilk
- 2 tbsps. almonds chopped
- ¼ cup cherries
- 1 pinch sea salt
- 1/4 cup ice cubes

FOR TOPPING
- 2 oz. keto chocolate chips
- 2 oz. cherries
- 2 mini chaffles
- 2 scoop heavy cream, frozen

DIRECTIONS
1. Add almond milk, almonds, cherries, salt and ice in a blender, blend for 2 minutes until smooth and fluffy.
2. Pour the smoothie into glasses.

3. Top with one scoop heavy cream, chocolate chips, cherries and chaffle in each glass.
4. Serve and enjoy!

NUTRITIONAL INFORMATION

Amount per serving 141g

Total Calories	293 kcal
Fats	29.27 g
Protein	3.2 g
Net Carbs	0.46 g
Fiber	3.1 g
Starch	0.01 g

Protein: 4% 11 kcal
Fat: 84% 245 kcal
Carbohydrates: 13% 37 kcal

THANKSGIVING PUMPKIN LATTE
WITH CHAFFLES

Prep Time	5 min
Cooking time	5min
Total time	10 min
Servings	1

INGREDIENTS
- 3/4 cup unsweetened coconut milk
- 2 tbsps. Heavy cream
- 2 tbsps. Pumpkin puree
- 1 tsp. stevia
- 1/4 tsp pumpkin spice
- 1/4 tsp Vanilla extract
- 1/4 cup espresso

FOR TOPPING
- 2 scoop whipped cream
- Pumpkin spice
- 2 heart shape mini chaffles

DIRECTIONS

1. Mix together all recipe ingredients in mug and microwave for 1 minute.
2. Pour thelatte intoa serving glass.
3. Top with a heavy cream scoop, pumpkin spice, and chaffle.
4. Serve and enjoy!

NUTRITIONAL INFORMATION

Amount per serving 143 g

Total Calories	306 kcal
Fats	30.72 g
Protein	4.62 g
Net Carbs	1.09 g
Fiber	2.5 g
Starch	0.05 g

Protein: 5% 16 kcal
Fat: 85% 259 kcal
Carbohydrates: 10% 29 kcal

THANKSGIVING PUMPKIN SPICE CHAFFLE

Prep Time   5 min
Cooking time   5min
Total time   10 min
Servings   4

INGREDIENTS
- 1 cup egg whites
- ¼ cup pumpkin puree
- 2 tsps. pumpkin pie spice
- 2 tsps. coconut flour
- ½ tsp. vanilla
- 1 tsp. baking powder
- 1 tsp. baking soda
- 1/8 tsp cinnamon powder
- 1 cup mozzarella cheese, grated
- 1/2 tsp. garlic powder

DIRECTIONS
- Switch on your square waffle maker. Spray with non-stick spray.
- Beat egg whites with beater, until fluffy and white.
- Add pumpkin puree, pumpkin pie spice, coconut flour in egg whites and beat again.

- Stir in the cheese, cinnamon powder, garlic powder, baking soda, and powder.
- Pour ½ of the batter in the waffle maker.
- Close the maker and cook for about 3 minutes.
- Repeat with the remaining batter.
- Remove chaffles from the maker.
- Serve hot and enjoy!

NUTRITIONAL INFORMATION

Amount per serving 105 g

Total Calories	132 kcal
Fats	5.93 g
Protein	15.86 g
Net Carbs	1.61 g
Fiber	0.2g
Starch	0 g

Protein: 51% 66 kcal
Fat: 41% 53 kcal
Carbohydrates: 8% 10 kcal

CHAFFLE WITH CREAM TOPPING

Prep Time   5 min
Cooking time 5min
Total time   10 min
Servings   4

INGREDIENTS
- 1 cup egg whites
- ½ tsp. vanilla
- 1 tsp. baking powder
- 1 cup mozzarella cheese, grated

TOPPING
½ cup frozen heavy cream
Cherries

DIRECTIONS
- Switch on your square waffle maker. Spray with non-stick spray.
- Beat egg whites with beater, until fluffy and white.
- Stir in the cheese, baking powder and vanilla.
- Pour ½ of the batter in a waffle maker.
- Close the maker and cook for about 3 minutes.
- Repeat with the remaining batter.
- Remove chaffles from the maker.

- Serve with heavy cream and cherries on top and enjoy!

NUTRITIONAL INFORMATION

Amount per serving 221g

Total Calories	357 kcal
Fats	22.6 g
Protein	32.01 g
Net Carbs	2.34 g
Fiber	0.1g
Starch	0 g

Protein: 38% 133 kcal
Fat: 57% 201 kcal
Carbohydrates: 5% 18 kcal

EASTER MORNING SIMPLE CHAFFLES

Prep Time   5 min
Cooking time   5min
Total time   10 min
Servings   2

INGREDIENTS
- 1/2 cup egg whites
- 1 cup mozzarella cheese, melted

DIRECTIONS
1. Switch on your square waffle maker. Spray with non-stick spray.
2. Beat egg whites with beater, until fluffy and white.
3. Add cheese and mix well.
4. Pour batter in a waffle maker.
5. Close the maker and cook for about 3 minutes.
6. Repeat with the remaining batter.
7. Remove chaffles from the maker.
8. Serve hot and enjoy!

NUTRITIONAL INFORMATION

Amount per serving 42 g

Total Calories	120 kcal
Fats	7.9 g
Protein	10.42 g
Net Carbs	0.93 g
Fiber	0 g
Starch	0 g

Protein: 36% 42 kcal
Fat: 60% 71 kcal
Carbohydrates: 4% 5 kcal

CHRISTMAS MORNING CHOCO CHAFFLE CAKE

Prep Time   5 min
Cooking time   5min
Total time   10 min
Servings   8

INGREDIENTS
- 8 keto chocolate square chaffles
- 2 cups peanut butter
- 16 oz. raspberries

DIRECTIONS
1. Assemble chaffles in layers.
2. Spread peanut butter in each layer.
3. Top with raspberries.
4. Enjoy cake on Christmas morning with keto coffee!

NUTRITIONAL INFORMATION

Amount per serving 112 g

Total Calories	243kcal
Fats	42.44.72 g
Protein	7.87g
Net Carbs	1.67 g
Fiber	0 g
Starch	0 g

Protein: 3% 15 Kcal
Fat: 94% 207 Kcal
Carbohydrates: 3% 15 Kcal

HOLIDAYS CHAFFLES

Prep Time   5 min
Cooking time   5min
Total time   10 min
Servings   4

INGREDIENTS
- 1 cup egg whites
- 2 tsps. coconut flour
- ½ tsp. vanilla
- 1 tsp. baking powder
- 1 tsp. baking soda
- 1/8 tsp cinnamon powder
- 1 cup mozzarella cheese, grated

TOPPING
- Cranberries
- keto Chocolate sauce

DIRECTIONS
1. Make 4 mini chaffles from the chaffle ingredients.
2. Top with chocolate sauce and cranberries
3. Serve hot and enjoy!

NUTRITIONAL INFORMATION

Amount per serving 221g

Total Calories	357 kcal
Fats	22.6 g
Protein	32.01 g
Net Carbs	2.34 g
Fiber	0.1g
Starch	0 g

Protein: 38% 133 kcal
Fat: 57% 201 kcal
Carbohydrates: 5% 18 kcal

CHAPTER-9:
SAVORY CHAFFLE RECIPES

SPINACH CHAFFLES

Prep Time   5 min
Cooking time   5min
Total time   10 min
Servings   2

INGREDIENTS
- 1 cup egg whites
- 1 tsp. Italian spice
- 1 cup mozzarella cheese, grated
- 1/2 tsp. garlic powder
- 1 cup chopped spinach

DIRECTIONS
1. Switch on your square waffle maker. Spray with non-stick spray.
2. Beat egg whites with beater, until fluffy and white.
3. Mix together all ingredients in a blender.
4. Pour the batter in waffle maker over chopped spinach
5. Close the maker and cook for about 4-5 minutes.
6. Remove chaffles from the maker.
7. Serve hot and enjoy!

NUTRITIONAL INFORMATION

Amount per serving 139 g

Total Calories	173 kcal
Fats	7.71 g
Protein	21.31 g
Net Carbs	2.02g
Fiber	0.3 g
Starch	0 g

Protein: 52% 88 kcal
Fat: 41% 69 kcal
Carbohydrates: 7% 12 kcal

ZUCCHINI CHAFFLES WITH PEANUT BUTTER

Prep Time: 5 min
Cooking Time: 5 min
Total Time: 10 min
Servings: 2

INGREDIENTS
- 1 cup zucchini grated
- 1 egg beaten
- 1/2 cup shredded parmesan cheese
- 1/4 cup shredded mozzarella cheese
- 1 tsp dried basil
- 1/2 tsp. salt
- 1/2 tsp. black pepper
- 2 tbsps. peanut butter for topping

DIRECTIONS
1. Sprinkle salt over zucchini and let it sit for 10 minutes.
2. Squeeze out water from zucchini.
3. Beat egg with zucchini, basil. saltmozzarella cheese, and pepper.
4. Sprinkle ½ of the parmesan cheese over preheated waffle maker and pour zucchini batter over it.

5. Sprinkle the remaining cheese over it.
6. Close the lid.
7. Cook zucchini chaffles for about 4-8 minutes.
8. Remove chaffles from the maker and repeat with the remaining batter.
9. Serve with peanut butter on top and enjoy!

NUTRITIONAL INFORMATION

Amount per serving 139 g

Total Calories	173 kcal
Fats	7.71 g
Protein	21.31 g
Net Carbs	2.02g
Fiber	0.3 g
Starch	0 g

Protein: 52% 88 kcal
Fat: 41% 69 kcal
Carbohydrates: 7% 12 kcal

SAVORY BAGEL SEASONING CHAFFLES

Prep Time: 5 min
Cooking Time: 5 min
Total Time: 10 min
Servings: 4

INGREDIENTS

- 2 tbsps. everything bagel seasoning
- 2 eggs
- 1 cup mozzarella cheese
- 1/2 cup grated parmesan

DIRECTIONS

1. Preheat the square waffle maker and grease with cooking spray.
2. Mix together eggs, mozzarella cheese and grated cheese in a bowl.
3. Pour half of the batter in the waffle maker.
4. Sprinkle 1 tbsp. of the everything bagel seasoning over batter.
5. Close the lid.
6. Cook chaffles for about 3-4 minutes.
7. Repeat with the remaining batter.
8. Serve hot and enjoy!

NUTRITIONAL INFORMATION

Amount per serving 81 g

Total Calories	210 kcal
Fats	13.94 g
Protein	17.11 g
Net Carbs	2.53 g
Fiber	0 g
Starch	0 g

Protein: 34% 71 kcal
Fat: 60% 125 kcal
Carbohydrates: 6% 13 kcal

GARLIC AND SPINACH CHAFFLES

Prep Time   5 min
Cooking time   5min
Total time   10 min
Servings   2

INGREDIENTS
* 1 cup egg whites
* 1 tsp. Italian spice
* 2 tsps. coconut flour
* ½ tsp. vanilla
* 1 tsp. baking powder
* 1 tsp. baking soda
* 1 cup mozzarella cheese, grated
* 1/2 tsp. garlic powder
* 1 cup chopped spinach

DIRECTIONS
1. Switch on your square waffle maker. Spray with non-stick spray.
2. Beat egg whites with beater, until fluffy and white.
3. Add pumpkin puree, pumpkin pie spice, coconut flour in egg whites and beat again.
4. Stir in the cheese, powder, garlic powder, baking soda, and powder.

5. Sprinkle chopped spinach on a waffle maker
6. Pour the batter in waffle maker over chopped spinach
7. Close the maker and cook for about 4-5 minutes.
8. Remove chaffles from the maker.
9. Serve hot and enjoy!

NUTRITIONAL INFORMATION

Amount per serving 139 g

Total Calories	173 kcal
Fats	7.71 g
Protein	21.31 g
Net Carbs	2.02g
Fiber	0.3 g
Starch	0 g

Protein: 52% 88 kcal
Fat: 41% 69 kcal
Carbohydrates: 7% 12 kcal

CAULIFLOWER CHAFFLES

Prep Time   5 min
Cooking time   5min
Total time   10 min
Servings   2

INGREDIENTS
- 1 cup egg whites
- 1 cup mozzarella cheese, grated
- ½ cup cauliflower

DIRECTIONS
1. Switch on your square waffle maker. Spray with non-stick spray.
2. Mix together all ingredients in a blender.
3. Pour the batter in waffle maker over chopped spinach
4. Close the maker and cook for about 4-5 minutes.
5. Remove chaffles from the maker.
6. Serve hot and enjoy!

NUTRITIONAL INFORMATION

Amount per serving 205

Total Calories	210 kcal
Fats	7.19 g
Protein	20.24 g
Net Carbs	0.34 g
Fiber	0.5 g
Starch	0 g

Protein: 41% 87 kcal
Fat: 30% 63 kcal
Carbohydrates: 29% 60 kcal

CHAPTER-10:
VEGANCHAFFLE RECIPES

VEGAN CHAFFLES WITH FLAXSEED

Prep Time   5 min
Cooking time   5min
Total time   10 min
Servings   2

INGREDIENTS
- 1 tbsp. flaxseed meal
- 2 tbsps. warm water
- ¼ cup low carb vegan cheese
- ¼ cup chopped mint
- pinch of salt
- 2 oz. blueberries chunks

DIRECTIONS
1. Preheat waffle maker to medium-high heat and grease with cooking spray.
2. Mix together flaxseed meal and warm water and set aside to be thickened.
3. After 5 minutes' mix together all ingredients in flax egg.
4. Pour vegan waffle batter into the center of the waffle iron.
5. Close the waffle maker and let cook for 3-5 minutes
6. Once cooked, remove the vegan chaffle from the waffle maker and serve.

NUTRITIONAL INFORMATION

Amount per serving 70 g

Total Calories	130 kcal
Fats	42.44 g
Protein	10.1 g
Net Carbs	1.6 g
Fiber	1.4 g
Starch	0 g

Protein: 32% 42 kcal
Fat: 63% 82 kcal
Carbohydrates: 5% 6 kcal

ALMONDS AND FLAXSEEDS CHAFFLES

Prep Time   5 min
Cooking time   5min
Total time   10 min
Servings   2

INGREDIENTS
- 1/4 cup coconut flour
- 1 tsp. stevia
- 1 tbsp. ground flaxseed
- 1/4 tsp baking powder
- 1/2 cup almond milk
- 1/4 tsp vanilla extract
- 1/ cup low carb vegan cheese

DIRECTIONS
1. Mix together flaxseed in warm water and set aside.
2. Add in the remaining ingredients.
3. Switch on waffle iron and grease with cooking spray.
4. Pour the batter in the waffle machine and close the lid.
5. Cook the chaffles for about 3-4 minutes.
6. Once cooked, remove from the waffle machine.
7. Serve with berries and enjoy!

NUTRITIONAL INFORMATION

Amount per serving 70 g

Total Calories	130 kcal
Fats	42.44 g
Protein	10.1 g
Net Carbs	1.6 g
Fiber	1.4 g
Starch	0 g

Protein: 32% 42 kcal
Fat: 63% 82 kcal
Carbohydrates: 5% 6 kcal

VEGAN CHOCOLATE CHAFFLES

Prep Time   5 min
Cooking time   5min
Total time   10 min
Servings   2

INGREDIENTS
- 1/2 cupcoconut flour
- 3 tbsps. cocoa powder
- 2 tbsps. whole psyllium husk
- 1/2 teaspoon baking powder
- pinch of salt
- 1/2 cup vegan cheese, softened
- 1/4 cup coconut milk

DIRECTIONS
1. Prepare your waffle iron according to the manufacturer's instructions.
2. Mix together coconut flour, cocoa powder, baking powder, salt and husk in a bowl and set aside.
3. Add melted cheese and milk and mix well. Let it stand for a few minutes before cooking.
4. Pour batter in waffle machine and cook for about 3-4 minutes.
5. Once chaffles are cooked, carefully remove them from the waffle machine.
6. Serve with vegan icecream and enjoy!

NUTRITIONAL INFORMATION

Amount per serving 70 g

Total Calories	130 kcal
Fats	42.44 g
Protein	10.1 g
Net Carbs	1.6 g
Fiber	1.4 g
Starch	0 g

Protein: 32% 42 kcal
Fat: 63% 82 kcal
Carbohydrates: 5% 6 kcal

GARLIC MAYO VEGAN CHAFFLES

Prep Time   5 min
Cooking time   5min
Total time   10 min
Servings   2

INGREDIENTS
- 1 tbsp. chia seeds
- 2 ½ tbsps. water
- ¼ cup low carb vegan cheese
- 2 tbsps. coconut flour
- 1 cup low carb vegan cream cheese, softened
- 1 tsp. garlic powder
- pinch of salt
- 2 tbsps. vegan garlic mayo for topping

DIRECTIONS
1. Preheat your square waffle maker.
2. In a small bowl, mix chia seeds and water, let it stand for 5 minutes.
3. Add all ingredients to the chia seeds mixture and mix well.
4. Pour vegan chaffle batter in a greased waffle maker

5. Close the waffle maker and cook for about 3-5 minutes.
6. Once chaffles are cooked, remove from the maker.
7. Top with garlic mayo and pepper.
8. Enjoy!

NUTRITIONAL INFORMATION

Amount per serving 70 g

Total Calories	130 kcal
Fats	42.44 g
Protein	10.1 g
Net Carbs	1.6 g
Fiber	1.4 g
Starch	0 g

Protein: 32% 42 kcal
Fat: 63% 82 kcal
Carbohydrates: 5% 6 kcal

FRUITY VEGAN CHAFFLES

Prep Time   5 min
Cooking time   5min
Total time   10 min
Servings   2

INGREDIENTS
- 1 tbsp. chia seeds
- 2 tbsps. warm water
- ¼ cup low carb vegan cheese
- 2 tbsps. strawberry puree
- 2 tbsps. Greek yogurt
- pinch of salt

DIRECTIONS
1. Preheat mini waffle maker to medium-high heat.
2. In a small bowl, mix together chia seeds and water and let it stand for few minutes to be thickened.
3. Mix the rest of the ingredients in chia seed egg and mix well.
4. Spray waffle machine with cooking spray.
5. Pour vegan waffle batter into the center of the waffle iron.
6. Close the waffle maker and cook chaffles for about 3-5 minutes.
7. Once cooked, remove from the maker and serve with berries on top.

NUTRITIONAL INFORMATION

Amount per serving 70 g

Total Calories	130 kcal
Fats	42.44 g
Protein	10.1 g
Net Carbs	1.6 g
Fiber	1.4 g
Starch	0 g

Protein: 32% 42 kcal
Fat: 63% 82 kcal
Carbohydrates: 5% 6 kcal

CHAPTER-11:
CHAFFLE WITHOUT WAFFLE MAKER RECIPES

SIMPLE CHAFFLES WITHOUT MAKER

Prep Time   5 min
Cooking time   5min
Total time   10 min
Servings   2

INGREDIENTS
- 1 tbsp. chia seeds
- 1 egg
- 1/2 cup cheddar cheese
- pinch of salt
- 1 tbsp. avocado oil

DIRECTIONS
1. Heat your nonstick pan over medium heat
2. In a small bowl, mix together chia seeds, salt, egg, and cheese together
3. Grease pan with avocado oil.
4. Once the pan is hot, pour 2 tbsps. chaffle batter and cook for about 1-2 minutes.
5. Flip and cook for another 1-2 minutes.
6. Once chaffle is brown remove from pan.
7. Serve with berries on top and enjoy.

NUTRITIONAL INFORMATION

Amount per serving 62 g

Total Calories	227 kcal
Fats	20.25 g
Protein	10.7 g
Net Carbs	1.6 g
Fiber	1.4 g
Starch	0 g

Protein: 19% 44 kcal
Fat: 80% 181 kcal
Carbohydrates: 1% 2 kcal

ZUCCHINI CHAFFLES ON PAN

Prep Time   15 min
Cooking time   5min
Total time   20 min
Servings   4

INGREDIENTS
- 1 cup zucchini, grated
- 1 egg
- 1 cup cheddar cheese
- pinch of salt
- 1 tbsp. avocado oil

DIRECTIONS
1. Heat your nonstick pan over medium heat.
2. Pour salt over grated zucchini and let it sit for 5 minutes.
3. Remove water from zucchini
4. In a small bowl, mix zucchini, egg, and cheese together.
5. Grease pan with avocado oil.
6. Once the pan is hot, pour 2 tbsps. zucchini batter and cook for about 1-2 minutes.
7. Flip and cook for another 1-2 minutes.
8. Once the chaffle is brown, remove from pan.
9. Serve coconut cream on top and enjoy.

NUTRITIONAL INFORMATION

Amount per serving 57 g

Total Calories	198 kcal
Fats	17.08 g
Protein	10.25 g
Net Carbs	0.52 g
Fiber	0 g
Starch	0 g

Protein: 21% 42 kcal
Fat: 77% 153 kcal
Carbohydrates: 2% 3 kcal

PORK CHAFFLES ON PAN

Prep Time   15 min
Cooking time   5min
Total time   20 min
Servings   4

INGREDIENTS
- 1 cup pork, minced
- 1 egg
- ½ cup chopped parsley
- 1 cup cheddar cheese
- pinch of salt
- 1 tbsp. avocado oil

DIRECTIONS
1. Heat your nonstick pan over medium heat.
2. In a small bowl, mix together pork, parsley, egg, and cheese together
3. Grease pan with avocado oil.
4. Once the pan is hot, pour 2 tbsps. pork batter and cook for about 1-2 minutes.
5. Flip and cook for another 1-2 minutes.
6. Once chaffle is brown, remove from pan.
7. Serve BBQ sauce on top and enjoy!

NUTRITIONAL INFORMATION

Amount per serving 98 g

Total Calories	254 kcal
Fats	18.95 g
Protein	10.1 g
Net Carbs	1.6 g
Fiber	1.4 g
Starch	0 g

Protein: 31% 79 kcal
Fat: 67% 170 kcal
Carbohydrates: 2% 5 kcal

CAULIFLOWER CHAFFLES

Prep Time   15 min
Cooking time   5min
Total time   20 min
Servings   4

INGREDIENTS
- 1 cup cauliflower, chopped
- 1/2 cup egg whites
- 1 cup cheddar cheese
- pinch of salt
- 1 pinch garlic powder
- 1 pinch onion powder
- 1 tbsp. avocado oil

DIRECTIONS
1. Heat your nonstick pan over medium heat.
2. Blend all ingredients except oil in a blender.
3. Grease pan with avocado oil.
4. Once the pan is hot, pour 2 tbsps. cauliflower batter and cook for about 1-2 minutes.
5. Flip and cook for another 1-2 minutes.
6. Once the chaffle is brown, remove from pan.
7. Serve with garlic mayo on top and enjoy!

NUTRITIONAL INFORMATION

Amount per serving 94 g

Total Calories	189 kcal
Fats	14.79 g
Protein	11.83 g
Net Carbs	1.53 g
Fiber	0.6 g
Starch	0 g

Protein: 25% 48 kcal
Fat: 70% 133 kcal
Carbohydrates: 5% 9 kcal

SAVORY CHAFFLES

Prep Time   15 min
Cooking time   5min
Total time   20 min
Servings   4

INGREDIENTS

- **1** egg
- 1 cup cheddar cheese
- pinch of salt
- 2 green chillies, chopped
- 1 tsp. red chilli flakes
- 1/2 cup spinach chopped
- ½ cup cauliflower
- 1 pinch garlic powder
- 1 pinch onion powder
- 1 tbsp. coconut oil

DIRECTIONS

1. Heat your nonstick pan over medium heat.
2. Blend all ingredients except oil in a blender.
3. Grease pan with avocado oil.
4. Once the pan is hot, pour 2 tbsps. cauliflower batter and cook for about 1-2 minutes.

5. Flip and cook for another 1-2 minutes.
6. Once chaffle is brown, remove from pan.
7. Serve hot and enjoy!

NUTRITIONAL INFORMATION

Amount per serving 70 g

Total Calories	130 kcal
Fats	42.44 g
Protein	10.1 g
Net Carbs	1.6 g
Fiber	1.4 g
Starch	0 g

Protein: 32% 42 kcal
Fat: 63% 82 kcal
Carbohydrates: 5% 6 kcal

HEART SHAPE CHAFFLES

Prep Time   5 min
Cooking time   5 min
Total time   10 min
Servings   2

INGREDIENTS

- **1** egg
- 1 cup mozzarella cheese
- 1 tsp baking powder
- ¼ cup almond flour
- 1 tbsp. coconut oil

DIRECTIONS

1. Heat your nonstick pan over medium heat.
2. Mix together all ingredients in a bowl.
3. Grease pan with avocado oil and place a heart shape cookie cutter over the pan.
4. Once the pan is hot, pour the batter equally in 2 cutters.
5. Cook for another 1-2 minutes.
6. Once chaffle is set, remove the cutter, flip and cook for another 1-2 minutes.
7. Once chaffles are brown, remove from the pan.
8. Serve hot and enjoy!

NUTRITIONAL INFORMATION

Amount per serving 107 g

Total Calories	177 kcal
Fats	13.7 g
Protein	10.7 g
Net Carbs	1.13 g
Fiber	0.7 g
Starch	0 g

Protein: 24% 43 kcal
Fat: 69% 123 kcal
Carbohydrates: 6% 11 kcal

OVEN-BAKED CHAFFLES

Prep Time   5 min
Cooking time 5 min
Total time   10 min
Servings   10

INGREDIENTS

- **3** eggs
- 2 cups mozzarella cheese
- ¼ cup coconut flour
- 1 tsp. baking powder
- 1 tbsp. coconut oil
- 1 tsp stevia
- 1 tbsp. coconut cream

DIRECTIONS

Preheat oven on 400⁰ F.

1. Mix together all ingredients in a bowl.
2. Pour batter in silicon waffle mold and set it on a baking tray.
3. Bake chaffles in an oven for about 10-15 minutes.
4. Once cooked, remove from oven
5. Serve hot with coffee and enjoy!

NUTRITIONAL INFORMATION

Amount per serving 44 g

Total Calories	109 kcal
Fats	7.41 g
Protein	9.04 g
Net Carbs	1.50 g
Fiber	0.2 g
Starch	0 g

Protein: 34% 37 kcal
Fat: 61% 66 kcal
Carbohydrates: 5% 6 kcal

BROCCOLI CHAFFLES ON PAN

Prep Time   15 min
Cooking time   5 min
Total time   15 min
Servings   4

INGREDIENTS
- **1** egg
- 1 cup cheddar cheese
- ½ cup broccoli chopped
- 1 tsp baking powder
- 1 pinch garlic powder
- 1 pinch salt
- 1 pinch black pepper
- 1 tbsp. coconut oil

DIRECTIONS
1. Heat your nonstick pan over medium heat.
2. Mix together all ingredients in a bowl.
3. Grease pan with oil.
4. Once the pan is hot, pour broccoli and cheese batter on greased pan
5. Cook for 1-2 minutes.
6. Flip and cook for another 1-2 minutes.

7. Once chaffles are brown, remove from the pan.
8. Serve with raspberries and melted coconut oil on top.
9. Enjoy!

NUTRITIONAL INFORMATION

Amount per serving 73 g

Total Calories	196 kcal
Fats	16.03 g
Protein	10.07g
Net Carbs	1.29 g
Fiber	1.3 g
Starch	0 g

Protein: 20% 40 kcal
Fat: 72% 142 kcal
Carbohydrates: 7% 15 kcal

APPENDIX

CALORIES IN FOOD: CALORIE CHART DATABASE

Food Categories	Measure	Calories
MILK PRODUCTS		
Whole Milk	225 ml (1 cup)	150
Paneer (Whole Milk)	60 gms	150
Butter	1 tbsp	45
Ghee	1 tbsp	45
FRUITS		
Apple	1 small	50 - 60
Banana	1/2 medium	50 - 60
Grapes	15 small	50 - 60
Mango	1/2 small	50 - 60
Musambi	1 medium	50 - 60
Orange	1 medium	50 - 60
CEREALS		
Cooked Cereal	1/2 cup	80
Rice Cooked	25 gms	80
Chapatti	1 medium	80
STARCHY VEGETABLES		
Potato	1 medium	80
Dal	1 large katori	80
Mixed Vegetables	150 gms	80
PROTEIN / MEAT		
Fish	50 gms	55
Mutton	1 oz	75
Egg	1 item	75
Cooked Food		
Biscuit (Sweet)	15 gms	70
Cake (Plain)	50 gms	135
Cake (Rich Chocolate)	50 gms	225
Dosa (Plain)	1 medium	135
Dosa (Masala)	1 medium	250
Pakoras	50 gms	175
Puri	1 large	85
Samosa	1 piece	140
Vada (Medu)	1 small	70

MAIN DISHES		
Biryani (Mutton)	1 cup	225
Biryani (Veg.)	1 cup	200
Curry (Chicken)	100 gms	225
Curry (Veg.)	100 gms	130
Fried Fish	85 gms	140
Pulav (Veg.)	100 gms	130
SWEET DISHES		
Carrot Halwa	45 gms	165
Jalebi	20gms	100
Kheer	100 gms	180
Rasgulla	50 gms	140
BEVERAGES		
Beer	125 fl. oz	150
Cola	200 ml	90
Wine	3.5 fl. oz	85

KETOGENIC FOOD

SR.NO	FOOD TO EAT IN KETO DIET	FOOD TO AVOID IN KETO DIET
1	**VEGETABLES**	• Beans, peas, lentils, and peanuts

VEGETABLES

- Tomatoes
- Eggplant
- Asparagus
- Broccoli
- Cauliflower
- Leafy greens
- Cucumber
- Bell peppers
- Zucchini
- Celery
- Brussels sprouts

2 PROTEIN

- Chicken, dark meat if possible
- Turkey, dark meat if possible
- Venison
- Beef
- Fish and seafood, especially fatty fish like salmon, sardines, tuna Pork
- Lamb

FOOD TO AVOID IN KETO DIET

- Beans, peas, lentils, and peanuts
- Grains, such as rice, pasta, and oatmeal
- Low-fat dairy products
- Added sugars and sweeteners
- Sugary beverages, including juice and soda
- Traditional snack foods, such as potato chips, pretzels, and crackers
- Most fruits, except for lemons, limes, tomatoes, and small portions of berries
- Starchy vegetables, including corn, potatoes, and peas
- Trans fats, such as margarine or other hydrogenated fats

- Eggs
- Natural cheeses
- Unsweetened, whole milk plain Greek yogurt
- Whole milk ricotta cheese
- Whole milk cottage cheese
- Most alcohols, including wine, beer, and sweetened cocktails

3   **FATS**

- Olive oil
- Avocado oil
- Olives
- Avocados
- Flaxseeds
- Chia seeds
- Pumpkin seeds
- Sesame seeds
- Nuts

COOKING MEASUREMENT (CONVERSIONS)

CUPS		
1 cup flour	4oz.	110g
1 cup sugar (crystal or castor)	8oz.	230g
1 cup icing sugar (free of lumps)	5oz.	140g
1 cup shortening (butter, marg. etc.)	8oz.	230g
1 cup honey, golden syrup, treacle	10oz.	280g
1 cup brown sugar (lightly packed)	4oz.	110g
1 cup brown sugar (firmly packed)	5oz.	140g
1 cup soft breadcrumbs	2oz.	60g
1 cup dry packet breadcrumbs	4oz.	110g
1 cup rice (uncooked)	6oz.	170g
1 cup rice (cooked)	5oz.	140g
1 cup mixed fruit (sultanas etc.)	4oz.	110g
1 cup grated cheese	4oz.	110g
1 cup nuts (chopped)	4oz.	110g
1 cup coconut	2½oz.	71g
SPOONS (LEVEL TABLESPOONS)		
1 oz. flour	2	
1 oz. sugar (crystal or castor)	1½	
1 oz. icing sugar (free from lumps)	2	
1 oz. shortening	1	
1oz. honey	1	
1oz. gelatin	2	
1oz. cocoa	3	
1oz. corn flour	2½	
1oz. custard powder	2½	

LIQUID		
1 cup liquid	8oz.	230mls.
21/2 cups liquid	20oz.(1 pint)	575mls.
4 cups liquid	32oz.	1 liter
2 tablespoons liquid	1oz.	30mls.
1 gill liquid	5oz.(1/4 pint)	150mls.
METRIC		

cup measures listed use the 8 liquid ounce cup

spoon measures listed are ordinary household cutlery

2 teaspoons = 1 dessertspoon

2 dessertspoons = 1 tablespoon

4 teaspoons = 1 tablespoon

1 ounce = 28.352 gram. (for convenience work on 30grams)

1 lbs. = 453 grams <> 2.2 lbs. = 1Kg

2 pounds 3 ounces = 1 kilogram

CPSIA information can be obtained
at www.ICGtesting.com
Printed in the USA
BVHW061053230621
610291BV00003B/345

9 781803 003375